STATUTORY SUPPLEMENT

TO

ADMIRALTY AND MARITIME LAW IN THE UNITED STATES

STATUTORY SUPPLEMENT

TO

ADMIRALTY AND MARITIME LAW
IN THE UNITED STATES

Second Edition

David W. Robertson

W. Page Keeton Chair in Tort Law
University Distinguished Teaching Professor
University of Texas School of Law

Steven F. Friedell

Professor of Law
Rutgers University School of Law (Camden)

Michael F. Sturley

Stanley D. and Sandra J. Rosenberg Centennial Professor
University of Texas School of Law

CAROLINA ACADEMIC PRESS
Durham, North Carolina

ISBN: 978-1-59460-635-9

Carolina Academic Press
700 Kent Street
Durham, North Carolina 27701
Telephone (919) 489-7486
Fax (919) 493-5668
www.cap-press.com

Printed in the United States of America

Contents

Introduction

This *Statutory Supplement* is designed for use with our casebook, *Admiralty and Maritime Law in the United States* (2d ed. 2008), which is also published by Carolina Academic Press. It does not begin to include all of the statutory material that would be required to practice in the field, but it does include virtually all of the statutory material that a typical student would wish to consult in working through the teaching materials in the casebook. Each source begins with a brief introductory passage to put the material in context. Further information is available in the appropriate section of the casebook, or in standard references.

The statutory excerpts here could not be arranged in an order corresponding to the coverage in the casebook itself (*i.e.*, the statutory material relevant to chapter I preceding that relevant to chapter II, and so on), for the simple reason that most of the material included here is relevant in more than one section of the casebook. Indeed, the principal rationale for having the *Statutory Supplement* is to enable a student to refer to statutory authority when relevant without having to flip back and forth between different parts of the casebook, and without having to reprint the same provision in more than one part of the casebook.

Most of the *Statutory Supplement* consists of federal material, which is arranged in a hierarchical order — first the Constitutional provisions, then federal statutes, and finally federal rules. The federal statutes are, for the most part, arranged here in the same order that they have been codified in the United States Code. (Excerpts from the Federal Tort Claims Act, however, are reprinted together, starting on page 11.) The *Supplement* concludes with four international sources, which are arranged chronologically.

In editing these materials, we have used the same signals that we did in the casebook. Omitted text is signaled by three asterisks. Inserted text is enclosed in brackets. Our own editorial footnotes are marked as such.

STATUTORY SUPPLEMENT
TO
ADMIRALTY AND MARITIME LAW
IN THE UNITED STATES

United States Constitution

Selected provisions of the U.S. Constitution are reproduced here.

Article I, Section 8

The Congress shall have Power * * *

[clause 3, the Commerce Clause] To regulate Commerce with foreign Nations, and among the several States, and with the Indian Tribes;

* * *

[clause 9] To constitute Tribunals inferior to the supreme Court;

[clause 10] To define and punish Piracies and Felonies committed on the high Seas, and Offences against the Law of Nations;

[clause 11] To declare War, grant Letters of Marque and Reprisal, and make Rules concerning Captures on Land and Water;

* * *

[clause 18, the Necessary and Proper Clause] To make all Laws which shall be necessary and proper for carrying into Execution the foregoing Powers and all other Powers vested by this Constitution in the Government of the United States, or in any Department or Officer thereof.

Article III, Section 1

The judicial Power of the United States, shall be vested in one supreme Court, and in such inferior Courts as the Congress may from time to time ordain and establish. The Judges, both of the supreme and inferior Courts, shall hold their Offices during good Behaviour, and shall, at stated Times, receive for their Services, a Compensation, which shall not be diminished during their Continuance in Office.

Article III, Section 2

The judicial Power shall extend to all Cases, in Law and Equity, arising under this Constitution, the Laws of the United States, and Treaties made, or which shall be made, under their Authority;—to all Cases affecting Ambassadors, other public ministers and Consuls;—to all Cases of admiralty and maritime Jurisdiction;—to Controversies to which the United States shall be a Party;—to Controversies between two or more States;—between a State and Citizens of another State;—between Citizens of different States;—between Citizens of the same State claiming Lands under Grants of different States, and between a State, or the Citizens thereof, and foreign States, Citizens or Subjects.

In all Cases affecting Ambassadors, other public Ministers and Consuls, and those in which a State shall be Party, the supreme Court shall have original Jurisdiction. In all the other Cases before mentioned, the supreme Court shall have appellate Jurisdiction, both as to Law and Fact, with such Exceptions, and under such Regulations as the Congress shall make.

The Trial of all Crimes, except in Cases of Impeachment, shall be by Jury; and such Trial shall be held in the State where the said Crimes shall have been committed; but when not committed within any State, the Trial shall be at such Place or Places as the Congress may by Law have directed.

Article VI, Clause 2 (the Supremacy Clause)

This Constitution, and the Laws of the United States which shall be made in Pursuance thereof; and all Treaties made, or which shall be made, under the Authority of the United States, shall be the supreme Law of the Land; and the Judges in every State shall be bound thereby, any Thing in the Constitution or Laws of any state to the Contrary notwithstanding.

Amendment VII

In Suits at common law, where the value in controversy shall exceed twenty dollars, the right of trial by jury shall be preserved, and no fact tried by a jury, shall be otherwise re-examined in any Court of the United States, than according to the rules of the common law.

Amendment X

The powers not delegated to the United States by the Constitution, nor prohibited by it to the States, are reserved to the States respectively, or to the people.

Amendment XI

The Judicial power of the United States shall not be construed to extend to any suit in law or equity, commenced or prosecuted against one of the United States by Citizens of another State, or by Citizens or Subjects of any Foreign State.

Federal Statutory Material

Rules of Construction Act

The Rules of Construction Act is the first chapter of the United States Code. Congress enacted all of Title 1 into positive law in 1947, 61 Stat. 633, but the substance of these provisions goes back much further. Section 1 (which establishes a few general rules of construction and several definitions) is substantially the same as section 1 of the Revised Statutes of 1873. Section 3 (which defines "vessel") reenacts section 3 of the Revised Statutes, and similar definitions had been passed in 1866 and 1870.

Section 3 is self-evidently relevant in maritime law. Section 1 is relevant in the present context primarily for the introductory phrase (which makes context relevant). By its terms, this phrase applies only to section 1, but there is good reason to believe that it properly applies to the entire Rules of Construction Act (including 1 U.S.C. § 3).

1 U.S.C. § 1. Words denoting number, gender, and so forth

In determining the meaning of any Act of Congress, unless the context indicates otherwise —

words importing the singular include and apply to several persons, parties, or things;

words importing the plural include the singular;

words importing the masculine gender include the feminine as well;

words used in the present tense include the future as well as the present;

* * *

1 U.S.C. § 3. "Vessel" as including all means of water transportation

The word "vessel" includes every description of watercraft or other artificial contrivance used, or capable of being used, as a means of transportation on water.

Federal Judicial Code

The subject matter of the Federal Judicial Code, Title 28 of the United States Code, can be traced back to the first Judiciary Act, which was enacted by the First Congress in 1789. Indeed, the language of section 9 of that seminal Act remains so important that it is included in these materials after 28 U.S.C. § 1333, its modern counterpart. In 1948, Congress enacted Title 28 as positive law. 62 Stat. 869. Subsequent amendments have accordingly been to the authoritative text of the United States Code. Selected provisions of the Code are reproduced here.

28 U.S.C. § 1292. Interlocutory decisions

(a) Except as provided in subsections (c) and (d) of this section, the courts of appeals shall have jurisdiction of appeals from:

(1) Interlocutory orders of the district courts of the United States, the United States District Court for the District of the Canal Zone, the District Court of Guam, and the District Court of the Virgin Islands, or of the judges thereof, granting, continuing, modifying, refusing or dissolving injunctions, or refusing to dissolve or modify injunctions, except where a direct review may be had in the Supreme Court;

* * *

(3) Interlocutory decrees of such district courts or the judges thereof determining the rights and liabilities of the parties to admiralty cases in which appeals from final decrees are allowed.

(b) When a district judge, in making in a civil action an order not otherwise appealable under this section, shall be of the opinion that such order involves a controlling question of law as to which there is substantial ground for difference of opinion and that an immediate appeal from the order may materially advance the ultimate termination of the litigation, he shall so state in writing in such order. The Court of Appeals which would have jurisdiction of an appeal of such action may thereupon, in its discretion, permit an appeal to be taken from such order, if application is made to it within ten days after the entry of the order: *Provided, however,* That application for an appeal hereunder shall not stay proceedings in the district court unless the district judge or the Court of Appeals or a judge thereof shall so order.

* * *

28 U.S.C. § 1331. Federal question

The district courts shall have original jurisdiction of all civil actions arising under the Constitution, laws, or treaties of the United States.

28 U.S.C. § 1332. Diversity of citizenship; amount in controversy; costs

(a) The district courts shall have original jurisdiction of all civil actions where the matter in controversy exceeds the sum or value of $75,000, exclusive of interest and costs, and is between—

(1) citizens of different States;

(2) citizens of a State and citizens or subjects of a foreign state;

(3) citizens of different States and in which citizens or subjects of a foreign state are additional parties; and

(4) a foreign state, defined in [28 U.S.C. § 1603(a)], as plaintiff and citizens of a State or of different States.

For the purposes of this section, section 1335, and section 1441, an alien admitted to the United States for permanent residence shall be deemed a citizen of the State in which such alien is domiciled.

* * *

(c) For the purposes of this section and [28 U.S.C. § 1441]—

(1) a corporation shall be deemed to be a citizen of any State by which it has been incorporated and of the State where it has its principal place of business * * *.

* * *

28 U.S.C. § 1333. Admiralty, maritime and prize cases

The district courts shall have original jurisdiction, exclusive of the courts of the States, of:

(1) Any civil case of admiralty or maritime jurisdiction, saving to suitors in all cases all other remedies to which they are otherwise entitled.

(2) Any prize brought into the United States and all proceedings for the condemnation of property taken as prize.

First Judiciary Act, § 9, 1 Stat. 77 (1789) (current version codified at 28 U.S.C. § 1333).

The district courts shall have, exclusively of the courts of the several States, cognizance of all crimes and offences that shall be cognizable under the authority of the United States, committed within their respective districts, or upon the high seas; where no other punishment than whipping, not exceeding thirty stripes, a fine not exceeding one hundred dollars, or a term of imprisonment not exceeding six months, is to be inflicted; and shall also have exclusive original cognizance of all civil causes of admiralty and maritime jurisdiction, including all seizures under laws of impost, navigation or trade of the United States, where the seizures are made, on waters which are navigable from the sea by vessels of ten or more tons burthen, within their respective districts as well as upon the high seas; saving to suitors, in all cases, the right of a common law remedy, where the common law is competent to give it; and shall also have exclusive original cognizance of all seizures on land, or other waters than as aforesaid, made, and of all suits for penalties and forfeitures incurred, under the laws of the United States. And shall also have cognizance, concurrent with the courts of the several States, or the circuit courts, as the case may be, of all causes where an alien sues for a tort only in violation of the law of nations or a treaty of the United States. And shall also have cognizance, concurrent as last mentioned, of all suits at common law where the United States sue, and the matter in dispute amounts, exclusive of costs, to the sum or value of one hundred dollars. And shall also have jurisdiction exclusively of the courts of the several States, of all suits against consuls or vice-consuls, except for offences above the description aforesaid. And the trial of issues in fact, in the district courts, in all causes except civil causes of admiralty and maritime jurisdiction, shall be by jury.

28 U.S.C. § 1367. Supplemental jurisdiction

(a) Except as provided in subsections (b) and (c) or as expressly provided otherwise by Federal statute, in any civil action of which the district courts have original jurisdiction, the district courts shall have supplemental jurisdiction over all other claims that are so related to claims in the action within such original jurisdiction that they form part of the same case or controversy under Article III of the United States Constitution. Such supplemental jurisdiction shall include claims that involve the joinder or intervention of additional parties.

(b) In any civil action of which the district courts have original jurisdiction founded solely on [28 U.S.C. § 1332], the district courts shall not have supplemental jurisdiction under subsection (a) over claims by plaintiffs against persons made parties under Rule 14, 19, 20, or 24 of the Federal Rules of Civil Procedure, or over claims by persons proposed to be joined as plaintiffs under Rule 19 of such rules, or seeking to intervene as plaintiffs under Rule 24 of such rules, when exercising supplemental jurisdiction over such claims would be inconsistent with the jurisdictional requirements of section 1332.

(c) The district courts may decline to exercise supplemental jurisdiction over a claim under subsection (a) if—

(1) the claim raises a novel or complex issue of State law,

(2) the claim substantially predominates over the claim or claims over which the district court has original jurisdiction,

(3) the district court has dismissed all claims over which it has original jurisdiction, or

(4) in exceptional circumstances, there are other compelling reasons for declining jurisdiction.

* * *

28 U.S.C. § 1404(a). [Change of venue]

For the convenience of parties and witnesses, in the interest of justice, a district court may transfer any civil action to any other district or division where it might have been brought.

28 U.S.C. § 1406(a). [Cure or waiver of defects]

The district court of a district in which is filed a case laying venue in the wrong division or district shall dismiss, or if it be in the interest of justice, transfer such case to any district or division in which it could have been brought.

28 U.S.C. § 1441. Actions removable generally

(a) Except as otherwise expressly provided by Act of Congress, any civil action brought in a State court of which the district courts of the United States have original jurisdiction, may be removed by the defendant or the defendants, to the district court of the United States for the district and division embracing the place where such action is pending. For purposes of removal under this chapter,[1] the citizenship of defendants sued under fictitious names shall be disregarded.

(b) Any civil action of which the district courts have original jurisdiction founded on a claim or right arising under the Constitution, treaties or laws of the United States shall be removable without regard to the citizenship or residence of the parties. Any other such action shall be removable only if none of the parties in interest properly joined and served as defendants is a citizen of the State in which such action is brought.

* * *

---

1. Editors' note: The reference is to chapter 89 of Title 28, titled "District Courts; Removal of Cases from State Courts," 28 U.S.C. §§ 1441–52.

28 U.S.C. § 1445(a). Nonremovable actions

A civil action in any State court against a railroad or its receivers or trustees, arising under [Federal Employers Liability Act §§ 1–4, 5–10, 45 U.S.C. §§ 51–54, 55–60, *see infra* at 27], may not be removed to any district court of the United States.

28 U.S.C. § 2283. Stay of State court proceedings

A court of the United States may not grant an injunction to stay proceedings in a State court except as expressly authorized by Act of Congress, or where necessary in aid of its jurisdiction, or to protect or effectuate its judgments.

Federal Tort Claims Act

Congress originally enacted the Federal Tort Claims Act in 1946, 60 Stat. 842, and it was unofficially codified in the 1940 edition of Title 28 of the United States Code. Two years later, Congress enacted all of Title 28, including the Federal Tort Claims Act, as positive law. 62 Stat. 869 (1948). The Federal Tort Claims Act's provisions were concentrated in chapter 171, 28 U.S.C. §§ 2671–80, but a number of other sections—including all of those reproduced here—were based at least in part on the Act. Because Title 28 has been enacted as positive law, the original Act is essentially irrelevant today. Subsequent amendments to the Act's provisions, for example, have been to the authoritative Code text (without reference to the original Act). Here we reproduce the key Code provisions based on the Federal Tort Claims Act in one place so that they may be considered together.

28 U.S.C. § 1346(b)(1). [United States as defendant]

Subject to the provisions of chapter 171 of this title,[1] the district courts, together with the United States District Court for the District of the Canal Zone and the District Court of the Virgin Islands, shall have exclusive jurisdiction of civil actions on claims against the United States, for money damages, accruing on and after January 1, 1945, for injury or loss of property, or personal injury or death caused by the negligent or wrongful act or omission of any employee of the Government while acting within the scope of his office or employment, under circumstances where the United States, if a private person, would be liable to the claimant in accordance with the law of the place where the act or omission occurred.

28 U.S.C. § 1402(b). [United States as defendant]

Any civil action on a tort claim against the United States under [28 U.S.C. § 1346(b)] may be prosecuted only in the judicial district where the plaintiff resides or wherein the act or omission complained of occurred.

28 U.S.C. § 2401(b). [Time for commencing action against United States]

A tort claim against the United States shall be forever barred unless it is presented in writing to the appropriate Federal agency within two years after such claim accrues or unless action is begun within six months after the date of mailing, by certified or registered mail, of notice of final denial of the claim by the agency to which it was presented.

28 U.S.C. § 2402. Jury trial in actions against United States

Subject to chapter 179 of this title,[2] any action against the United States under section 1346 shall be tried by the court without a jury, except that any action against the United States under section 1346(a)(1)[3] shall, at the request of either party to such action, be tried by the court with a jury.

---

1. Editors' note: The reference is to chapter 171 of Title 28, titled "Tort Claims Procedure," 28 U.S.C. §§ 2671–80.
2. Editors' note: The reference is to chapter 179 of Title 28, titled "Judicial Review Of Certain Actions By Presidential Offices," 28 U.S.C. §§ 3901–08.
3. Editors' note: 28 U.S.C. § 1346(a)(1) confers jurisdiction on the district courts in tax refund cases.

28 U.S.C. § 2671. Definitions

As used in this chapter[4] and [28 U.S.C. §§ 1346(b), 2401(b)], the term "Federal agency" includes the executive departments, the judicial and legislative branches, the military departments, independent establishments of the United States, and corporations primarily acting as instrumentalities or agencies of the United States, but does not include any contractor with the United States.

"Employee of the government" includes (1) officers or employees of any federal agency, members of the military or naval forces of the United States, members of the National Guard while engaged in training or duty under [32 U.S.C. §§ 316, 502, 503, 504, or 505], and persons acting on behalf of a federal agency in an official capacity, temporarily or permanently in the service of the United States, whether with or without compensation, and (2) any officer or employee of a Federal public defender organization, except when such officer or employee performs professional services in the course of providing representation under [18 U.S.C. § 3006A[5]].

"Acting within the scope of his office or employment", in the case of a member of the military or naval forces of the United States or a member of the National Guard as defined in [32 U.S.C. § 101(3)], means acting in line of duty.

28 U.S.C. § 2672. Administrative adjustment of claims

The head of each Federal agency or his designee, in accordance with regulations prescribed by the Attorney General, may consider, ascertain, adjust, determine, compromise, and settle any claim for money damages against the United States for injury or loss of property or personal injury or death caused by the negligent or wrongful act or omission of any employee of the agency while acting within the scope of his office or employment, under circumstances where the United States, if a private person, would be liable to the claimant in accordance with the law of the place where the act or omission occurred: *Provided*, That any award, compromise, or settlement in excess of $25,000 shall be effected only with the prior written approval of the Attorney General or his designee. * * *

28 U.S.C. § 2674. Liability of United States

The United States shall be liable, respecting the provisions of this title relating to tort claims, in the same manner and to the same extent as a private individual under like circumstances, but shall not be liable for interest prior to judgment or for punitive damages.

If, however, in any case wherein death was caused, the law of the place where the act or omission complained of occurred provides, or has been construed to provide, for damages only punitive in nature, the United States shall be liable for actual or compensatory damages, measured by the pecuniary injuries resulting from such death to the persons respectively, for whose benefit the action was brought, in lieu thereof.

With respect to any claim under this chapter,[6] the United States shall be entitled to assert any defense based upon judicial or legislative immunity which otherwise would have been available to the employee of the United States whose act or omission gave rise to the claim, as well as any other defenses to which the United States is entitled.

* * *

---

4. Editors' note: The reference is to chapter 171 of Title 28, titled "Tort Claims Procedure," 28 U.S.C. §§ 2671–80.

5. Editors' note: 18 U.S.C. § 3006A deals with the representation of indigent criminal defendants.

6. Editors' note: The reference is to chapter 171 of Title 28, titled "Tort Claims Procedure," 28 U.S.C. §§ 2671–80.

28 U.S.C. § 2675. Disposition by federal agency as prerequisite; evidence

(a) An action shall not be instituted upon a claim against the United States for money damages for injury or loss of property or personal injury or death caused by the negligent or wrongful act or omission of any employee of the Government while acting within the scope of his office or employment, unless the claimant shall have first presented the claim to the appropriate Federal agency and his claim shall have been finally denied by the agency in writing and sent by certified or registered mail. The failure of an agency to make final disposition of a claim within six months after it is filed shall, at the option of the claimant any time thereafter, be deemed a final denial of the claim for purposes of this section. The provisions of this subsection shall not apply to such claims as may be asserted under the Federal Rules of Civil Procedure by third party complaint, cross-claim, or counterclaim.

(b) Action under this section shall not be instituted for any sum in excess of the amount of the claim presented to the federal agency, except where the increased amount is based upon newly discovered evidence not reasonably discoverable at the time of presenting the claim to the federal agency, or upon allegation and proof of intervening facts, relating to the amount of the claim.

(c) Disposition of any claim by the Attorney General or other head of a federal agency shall not be competent evidence of liability or amount of damages.

28 U.S.C. § 2676. Judgment as bar

The judgment in an action under [28 U.S.C. § 1346(b)] shall constitute a complete bar to any action by the claimant, by reason of the same subject matter, against the employee of the government whose act or omission gave rise to the claim.

28 U.S.C. § 2677. Compromise

The Attorney General or his designee may arbitrate, compromise, or settle any claim cognizable under [28 U.S.C. § 1346(b)], after the commencement of an action thereon.

28 U.S.C. § 2678. Attorney fees; penalty

No attorney shall charge, demand, receive, or collect for services rendered, fees in excess of 25 per centum of any judgment rendered pursuant to [28 U.S.C. § 1346(b)] or any settlement made pursuant to [28 U.S.C. § 2677], or in excess of 20 per centum of any award, compromise, or settlement made pursuant to [28 U.S.C. § 2672].

Any attorney who charges, demands, receives, or collects for services rendered in connection with such claim any amount in excess of that allowed under this section, if recovery be had, shall be fined not more than $2,000 or imprisoned not more than one year, or both.

28 U.S.C. § 2679. Exclusiveness of remedy

(a) The authority of any federal agency to sue and be sued in its own name shall not be construed to authorize suits against such federal agency on claims which are cognizable under [28 U.S.C. § 1346(b)], and the remedies provided by this title in such cases shall be exclusive.

(b)(1) The remedy against the United States provided by [28 U.S.C. §§ 1346(b) & 2672] for injury or loss of property, or personal injury or death arising or resulting from the negligent or wrongful act or omission of any employee of the Government while acting within the scope of his office or employment is exclusive of any other civil action or proceeding for money damages by reason of the same subject matter against the employee whose act or omission gave rise to the claim or against the estate of such employee. Any other civil action or proceeding for money damages arising out of or relating to the same subject matter against the employee or the employee's estate is precluded without regard to when the act or omission occurred.

(2) Paragraph (1) does not extend or apply to a civil action against an employee of the Government—

(A) which is brought for a violation of the Constitution of the United States, or

(B) which is brought for a violation of a statute of the United States under which such action against an individual is otherwise authorized.

(c) The Attorney General shall defend any civil action or proceeding brought in any court against any employee of the Government or his estate for any such damage or injury. * * *

(d)(1) Upon certification by the Attorney General that the defendant employee was acting within the scope of his office or employment at the time of the incident out of which the claim arose, any civil action or proceeding commenced upon such claim in a United States district court shall be deemed an action against the United States under the provisions of this title and all references thereto, and the United States shall be substituted as the party defendant.

(2) Upon certification by the Attorney General that the defendant employee was acting within the scope of his office or employment at the time of the incident out of which the claim arose, any civil action or proceeding commenced upon such claim in a State court shall be removed without bond at any time before trial by the Attorney General to the district court of the United States for the district and division embracing the place in which the action or proceeding is pending. Such action or proceeding shall be deemed to be an action or proceeding brought against the United States under the provisions of this title and all references thereto, and the United States shall be substituted as the party defendant. This certification of the Attorney General shall conclusively establish scope of office or employment for purposes of removal.

* * *

(4) Upon certification, any action or proceeding subject to paragraph (1), (2), or (3) shall proceed in the same manner as any action against the United States filed pursuant to [28 U.S.C. § 1346(b)] and shall be subject to the limitations and exceptions applicable to those actions.

* * *

28 U.S.C. § 2680. Exceptions

The provisions of this chapter[7] and [28 U.S.C. § 1346(b)] shall not apply to—

(a) Any claim based upon an act or omission of an employee of the Government, exercising due care, in the execution of a statute or regulation, whether or not such statute or regulation be valid, or based upon the exercise or performance or the failure to exercise or perform a discretionary function or duty on the part of a federal agency or an employee of the Government, whether or not the discretion involved be abused.

(b) Any claim arising out of the loss, miscarriage, or negligent transmission of letters or postal matter.

---

7. Editors' note: The reference is to chapter 171 of Title 28, titled "Tort Claims Procedure," 28 U.S.C. §§ 2671–80.

(c) Any claim arising in respect of the assessment or collection of any tax or customs duty, or the detention of any goods, merchandise, or other property by any officer of customs or excise or any other law enforcement officer * * * .

(d) Any claim for which a remedy is provided by [the Suits in Admiralty Act, 46 U.S.C. §§ 30901–18 (previously codified at 46 U.S.C. app. §§ 741–752), *infra* at 53, or the Public Vessels Act, 46 U.S.C. §§ 31101–13 (previously codified at 46 U.S.C. app. §§ 781–790), *infra* at 57], relating to claims or suits in admiralty against the United States.

(e) Any claim arising out of an act or omission of any employee of the Government in administering the provisions of [the Trading With the Enemy Act of 1917, 50 U.S.C. app. §§ 1–31].

(f) Any claim for damages caused by the imposition or establishment of a quarantine by the United States.

[(g) Repealed.]

(h) Any claim arising out of assault, battery, false imprisonment, false arrest, malicious prosecution, abuse of process, libel, slander, misrepresentation, deceit, or interference with contract rights: *Provided*, That, with regard to acts or omissions of investigative or law enforcement officers of the United States Government, the provisions of this chapter[8] and [28 U.S.C. § 1346(b)] shall apply to any claim arising, on or after the date of the enactment of this proviso, out of assault, battery, false imprisonment, false arrest, abuse of process, or malicious prosecution. For the purpose of this subsection, "investigative or law enforcement officer" means any officer of the United States who is empowered by law to execute searches, to seize evidence, or to make arrests for violations of Federal law.

(i) Any claim for damages caused by the fiscal operations of the Treasury or by the regulation of the monetary system.

(j) Any claim arising out of the combatant activities of the military or naval forces, or the Coast Guard, during time of war.

(k) Any claim arising in a foreign country.

(l) Any claim arising from the activities of the Tennessee Valley Authority.

(m) Any claim arising from the activities of the Panama Canal Company.

(n) Any claim arising from the activities of a Federal land bank, a Federal intermediate credit bank, or a bank for cooperatives.

---

8. Editors' note: The reference is to chapter 171 of Title 28, titled "Tort Claims Procedure," 28 U.S.C. §§ 2671–80.

Longshore and Harbor Workers' Compensation Act

Congress originally enacted the Longshoremen's and Harbor Workers' Compensation Act (LHWCA), 33 U.S.C. §§ 901–950, in 1927. 44 Stat. 1424. It has since amended the Act several times. See, e.g., Longshore and Harbor Workers' Compensation Act Amendments of 1984, 98 Stat. 1639; Longshoremen's and Harbor Workers' Compensation Act Amendments of 1972, 86 Stat. 1251. The Act acquired its current gender-neutral name as part of the 1984 Amendments. Selected provisions of the Act, as amended, are reproduced here.

LHWCA § 2, 33 U.S.C. § 902. Definitions

When used in this Act—

* * *

(2) The term "injury" means accidental injury or death arising out of and in the course of employment, and such occupational disease or infection as arises naturally out of such employment or as naturally or unavoidably results from such accidental injury, and includes an injury caused by the willful act of a third person directed against an employee because of his employment.

(3) The term "employee" means any person engaged in maritime employment, including any longshoreman or other person engaged in longshoring operations, and any harbor-worker including a ship repairman, shipbuilder, and ship-breaker, but such term does not include—

(A) individuals employed exclusively to perform office clerical, secretarial, security, or data processing work;

(B) individuals employed by a club, camp, recreational operation, restaurant, museum, or retail outlet;

(C) individuals employed by a marina and who are not engaged in construction, replacement, or expansion of such marina (except for routine maintenance);

(D) individuals who (i) are employed by suppliers, transporters, or vendors, (ii) are temporarily doing business on the premises of an employer described in paragraph (4), and (iii) are not engaged in work normally performed by employees of that employer under this Act;

(E) aquaculture workers;

(F) individuals employed to build, repair, or dismantle any recreational vessel under sixty-five feet in length;

(G) a master or member of a crew of any vessel; or

(H) any person engaged by a master to load or unload or repair any small vessel under eighteen tons net;

if individuals described in clauses (A) through (F) are subject to coverage under a State workers' compensation law.

(4) The term "employer" means an employer any of whose employees are employed in maritime employment, in whole or in part, upon the navigable waters of the United States (including any adjoining pier, wharf, dry dock, terminal, building way, marine railway,

or other adjoining area customarily used by an employer in loading, unloading, repairing, or building a vessel).

* * *

(21) Unless the context requires otherwise, the term "vessel" means any vessel upon which or in connection with which any person entitled to benefits under this Act suffers injury or death arising out of or in the course of his employment, and said vessel's owner, owner pro hac vice, agent, operator, charter [*sic*] or bare boat charterer, master, officer, or crew member.

LHWCA § 3, 33 U.S.C. § 903. Coverage.

(a) Except as otherwise provided in this section, compensation shall be payable under this Act in respect of disability or death of an employee, but only if the disability or death results from an injury occurring upon the navigable waters of the United States (including any adjoining pier, wharf, dry dock, terminal, building way, marine railway, or other adjoining area customarily used by an employer in loading, unloading, repairing, dismantling, or building a vessel).

(b) No compensation shall be payable in respect of the disability or death of an officer or employee of the United States, or any agency thereof, or of any State or foreign government, or any subdivision thereof.

(c) No compensation shall be payable if the injury was occasioned solely by the intoxication of the employee or by the willful intention of the employee to injure or kill himself or another.

* * *

(e) Notwithstanding any other provision of law, any amounts paid to an employee for the same injury, disability, or death for which benefits are claimed under this Act pursuant to any other workers' compensation law or [the Jones Act, 46 U.S.C. §§ 30104–05 (previously codified at 46 U.S.C. app. § 688), *infra* at 33] (relating to recovery for injury to or death of seamen), shall be credited against any liability imposed by this Act.

LHWCA § 4, 33 U.S.C. § 904. Liability for compensation.

(a) Every employer shall be liable for and shall secure the payment to his employees of the compensation payable under sections 7, 8, and 9 [33 U.S.C. §§ 907, 908, 909]. * * *

(b) Compensation shall be payable irrespective of fault as a cause for the injury.

LHWCA § 5, 33 U.S.C. § 905. [Exclusiveness of remedy; vessels' liability as third parties; Outer Continental Shelf]

(a) The liability of an employer prescribed in section 4 [33 U.S.C. § 904] shall be exclusive and in place of all other liability of such employer to the employee, his legal representative, husband or wife, parents, dependents, next of kin, and anyone otherwise entitled to recover damages from such employer at law or in admiralty on account of such injury or death, except that if an employer fails to secure payment of compensation as required by this Act, an injured employee, or his legal representative in case death results from the injury, may elect to claim compensation under the Act, or to maintain an action at law or in admiralty for damages on account of such injury or death. In such action the defendant may not plead as a defense that the injury was caused by the negligence of a fellow servant, or that the employee assumed the risk of his employment, or that the injury was due to the contributory negligence of the employee. * * *

(b) In the event of injury to a person covered under this Act caused by the negligence of a vessel, then such person, or anyone otherwise entitled to recover damages by reason thereof, may bring an action against such vessel as a third party in accordance with the provisions of section 33 of this Act [33 U.S.C. §933], and the employer shall not be liable to the vessel for such damages directly or indirectly and any agreements or warranties to the contrary shall be void. If such person was employed by the vessel to provide stevedoring services, no such action shall be permitted if the injury was caused by the negligence of persons engaged in providing stevedoring services to the vessel. If such person was employed to provide shipbuilding, repairing, or breaking services and such person's employer was the owner, owner pro hac vice, agent, operator, or charterer of the vessel, no such action shall be permitted, in whole or in part or directly or indirectly, against the injured person's employer (in any capacity, including as the vessel's owner, owner pro hac vice, agent, operator, or charterer) or against the employees of the employer. The liability of the vessel under this subsection shall not be based upon the warranty of seaworthiness or a breach thereof at the time the injury occurred. The remedy provided in this subsection shall be exclusive of all other remedies against the vessel except remedies available under this Act.

(c) In the event that the negligence of a vessel causes injury to a person entitled to receive benefits under this Act by virtue of section 4 of the Outer Continental Shelf Lands Act [43 U.S.C. §1333], then such person, or anyone otherwise entitled to recover damages by reason thereof, may bring an action against such vessel in accordance with the provisions of subsection (b) of this section. Nothing contained in subsection (b) of this section shall preclude the enforcement according to its terms of any reciprocal indemnity provision whereby the employer of a person entitled to receive benefits under this Act by virtue of section 4 of the Outer Continental Shelf Lands Act [43 U.S.C. §1333] and the vessel agree to defend and indemnify the other for cost of defense and loss or liability for damages arising out of or resulting from death or bodily injury to their employees.

LHWCA §33, 33 U.S.C. §933. Compensation for injuries where third persons are liable.

(a) If on account of a disability or death for which compensation is payable under this Act the person entitled to such compensation determines that some person other than the employer or a person or persons in his employ is liable in damages, he need not elect whether to receive such compensation or to recover damages against such third person.

(b) Acceptance of compensation under an award in a compensation order filed by the deputy commissioner, an administrative law judge, or the Board shall operate as an assignment to the employer of all rights of the person entitled to compensation to recover damages against such third person unless such person shall commence an action against such third person within six months after such acceptance. If the employer fails to commence an action against such third person within ninety days after the cause of action is assigned under this section, the right to bring such action shall revert to the person entitled to compensation. For the purpose of this subsection, the term "award" with respect to a compensation order means a formal order issued by the deputy commissioner, an administrative law judge, or Board.

* * *

(d) Such employer on account of such assignment may either institute proceedings for the recovery of such damages or may compromise with such third person either without or after instituting such proceeding.

(e) Any amount recovered by such employer on account of such assignment, whether or not as the result of a compromise, shall be distributed as follows:

(1) The employer shall retain an amount equal to—

(A) the expenses incurred by him in respect to such proceedings or compromise (including a reasonable attorney's fee as determined by the deputy commissioner or Board);

(B) the cost of all benefits actually furnished by him to the employee under section 7 [33 U.S.C. § 907];

(C) all amounts paid as compensation;

(D) the present value of all amounts thereafter payable as compensation, such present value to be computed in accordance with a schedule prepared by the Secretary, and the present value of the cost of all benefits thereafter to be furnished under section 7 [33 U.S.C. § 907], to be estimated by the deputy commissioner, and the amounts so computed and estimated to be retained by the employer as a trust fund to pay such compensation and the cost of such benefits as they become due, and to pay any sum finally remaining in excess thereof to the person entitled to compensation or to the representative; and

(2) The employer shall pay any excess to the person entitled to compensation or to the representative.

(f) If the person entitled to compensation institutes proceedings within the period prescribed in section 33(b) [33 U.S.C. § 933(b)] the employer shall be required to pay as compensation under this Act a sum equal to the excess of the amount which the Secretary determines is payable on account of such injury or death over the net amount recovered against such third person. Such net amount shall be equal to the actual amount recovered less the expenses reasonably incurred by such person in respect to such proceedings (including reasonable attorneys' fees).

(g)(1) If the person entitled to compensation (or the person's representative) enters into a settlement with a third person referred to in subsection (a) for an amount less than the compensation to which the person (or the person's representative) would be entitled under this Act, the employer shall be liable for compensation as determined under subsection (f) only if written approval of the settlement is obtained from the employer and the employer's carrier, before the settlement is executed, and by the person entitled to compensation (or the person's representative). The approval shall be made on a form provided by the Secretary and shall be filed in the office of the deputy commissioner within thirty days after the settlement is entered into.

(2) If no written approval of the settlement is obtained and filed as required by paragraph (1), or if the employee fails to notify the employer of any settlement obtained from or judgment rendered against a third person, all rights to compensation and medical benefits under this Act shall be terminated, regardless of whether the employer or the employer's insurer has made payments or acknowledged entitlement to benefits under this Act.

* * *

(h) Where the employer is insured and the insurance carrier has assumed the payment of the compensation, the insurance carrier shall be subrogated to all the rights of the employer under this section.

(i) The right to compensation or benefits under this Act shall be the exclusive remedy to an employee when he is injured, or to his eligible survivors or legal representatives if he is killed, by the negligence or wrong of any other person or persons in the same employ: *Provided,* That this provision shall not affect the liability of a person other than an officer or employee of the employer.

Outer Continental Shelf Lands Act

Congress originally enacted the Outer Continental Shelf Lands Act ("OCSLA"), 43 U.S.C. § 1331–56, in 1953. 67 Stat. 462. It has since amended the Act several times. See, e.g., Outer Continental Shelf Lands Act Amendments of 1985, 100 Stat. 147 (1986); Outer Continental Shelf Lands Act Amendments of 1978, 92 Stat. 629. Selected provisions of the Act, as amended, are reproduced here.

OCSLA § 2(a), 43 U.S.C. § 1331(a). Definitions.

When used in this Act—

(a) The term "outer Continental Shelf" means all submerged lands lying seaward and outside of the area of lands beneath navigable waters[1] as defined in [Submerged Lands Act § 2, 43 U.S.C. § 1301], and of which the subsoil and seabed appertain to the United States and are subject to its jurisdiction and control[.]

OCSLA § 3(1), 43 U.S.C. § 1332(1). [Congressional declaration of policy]

It is hereby declared to be the policy of the United States that—

(1) the subsoil and seabed of the outer Continental Shelf appertain to the United States and are subject to its jurisdiction, control, and power of disposition as provided in this Act[.]

OCSLA § 4, 43 U.S.C. § 1333. Laws Applicable to Outer Continental Shelf.

(a)(1) The Constitution and laws and civil and political jurisdiction of the United States are hereby extended to the subsoil and seabed of the outer Continental Shelf and to all artificial islands, and all installations and other devices permanently or temporarily attached to the seabed, which may be erected thereon for the purpose of exploring for, developing, or producing resources therefrom, or any such installation or other device (other than a ship or vessel) for the purpose of transporting such resources, to the same extent as if the outer Continental Shelf were an area of exclusive Federal jurisdiction located within a State: *Provided, however,* That mineral leases on the outer Continental Shelf shall be maintained or issued only under the provisions of this Act.

(2)(A) To the extent that they are applicable and not inconsistent with this Act or with other Federal laws and regulations of the Secretary [of the Interior] now in effect or hereafter adopted, the civil and criminal laws of each adjacent State, now in effect or hereafter adopted, amended, or repealed are declared to be the law of the United

---

1. Editors' note: The term "lands beneath navigable waters" is defined in Submerged Lands Act § 2(a), 43 U.S.C. § 1301(a), as:

(1) all lands within the boundaries of each of the respective States which are covered by nontidal waters that were navigable under the laws of the United States at the time such State became a member of the Union, or acquired sovereignty over such lands and waters thereafter, up to the ordinary high water mark as heretofore or hereafter modified by accretion, erosion, and reliction;

(2) all lands permanently or periodically covered by tidal waters up to but not above the line of mean high tide and seaward to a line three geographical miles distant from the coast line of each such State and to the boundary line of each such State where in any case such boundary as it existed at the time such State became a member of the Union, or as heretofore approved by Congress, extends seaward (or into the Gulf of Mexico) beyond three geographical miles, and

(3) all filled in, made, or reclaimed lands which formerly were lands beneath navigable waters, as hereinabove defined.

States for that portion of the subsoil and seabed of the outer Continental Shelf, and artificial islands and fixed structures erected thereon, which would be within the area of the State if its boundaries were extended seaward to the outer margin of the outer Continental Shelf, and the President shall determine and publish in the Federal Register such projected lines extending seaward and defining each such area. All of such applicable laws shall be administered and enforced by the appropriate officers and courts of the United States. State taxation laws shall not apply to the outer Continental Shelf.

* * *

(b) With respect to disability or death of an employee resulting from any injury occurring as the result of operations conducted on the outer Continental Shelf for the purpose of exploring for, developing, removing, or transporting by pipeline the natural resources, or involving rights to the natural resources, of the subsoil and seabed of the outer Continental Shelf, compensation shall be payable under the provisions of the Longshore and Harbor Workers' Compensation Act [33 U.S.C. §§ 901–950]. For the purposes of the extension of the provisions of the Longshore and Harbor Workers' Compensation Act under this section—

(1) the term "employee" does not include a master or member of a crew of any vessel, or an officer or employee of the United States or any agency thereof or of any State or foreign government, or of any political subdivision thereof;

(2) the term "employer" means an employer any of whose employees are employed in such operations; and

(3) the term "United States" when used in a geographical sense includes the outer Continental Shelf and artificial islands and fixed structures thereon.

* * *

OCSLA § 23(b)(1), 43 U.S.C. § 1349(b)(1). [Jurisdiction and venue of actions]

Except as provided in subsection (c) of this section [43 U.S.C. § 1349(c), which provides for judicial review in the United States Court of Appeals for the District of Columbia of the Secretary's approval of mineral leasing programs], the district courts of the United States shall have jurisdiction of cases and controversies arising out of, or in connection with (A) any operation conducted on the outer Continental Shelf which involves exploration, development, or production of the minerals, of the subsoil and seabed of the outer Continental Shelf, or which involves rights to such minerals, or (B) the cancellation, suspension, or termination of a lease or permit under this Act. Proceedings with respect to any such case or controversy may be instituted in the judicial district in which any defendant resides or may be found, or in the judicial district of the State nearest the place the cause of action arose.

Abandoned Shipwreck Act

Despite the date in its official "short title," Congress enacted the Abandoned Shipwreck Act of 1987, 43 U.S.C. §2101-06, in April of 1988. 102 Stat. 432. Selected provisions are reproduced here.

Abandoned Shipwreck Act §3, 43 U.S.C. §2102. Definitions.

For purposes of this Act—

(a) the term "embedded" means firmly affixed in the submerged lands or in coralline formations such that the use of tools of excavation is required in order to move the bottom sediments to gain access to the shipwreck, its cargo, and any part thereof;

(b) the term "National Register" means the National Register of Historic Places maintained by the Secretary of the Interior under [National Historic Preservation Act §101, 16 U.S.C. §470a];

(c) the terms "public lands", "Indian lands", and "Indian tribe" have the same meaning given the terms in the Archaeological [Resources] Protection Act of 1979 [16 U.S.C. §§470aa–470ll];

(d) the term "shipwreck" means a vessel or wreck, its cargo, and other contents;

(e) the term "State" means a State of the United States, the District of Columbia, Puerto Rico, Guam, the Virgin Islands, American Samoa, and the Northern Mariana Islands; and

(f) the term "submerged lands" means the lands—

(1) that are "lands beneath navigable waters,"[1] as defined in [Submerged Lands Act §2, 43 U.S.C. §1301];

(2) of Puerto Rico, as described in [48 U.S.C. §749];

(3) of Guam, the Virgin Islands and American Samoa, as described in [48 U.S.C. §1705]; and

(4) of the Commonwealth of the Northern Mariana Islands, as described in section 801 of Public Law 94-241.[2]

Abandoned Shipwreck Act §6, 43 U.S.C. §2105. Rights of ownership.

(a) **United States Title.** The United States asserts title to any abandoned shipwreck that is—

(1) embedded in submerged lands of a State;

(2) embedded in coralline formations protected by a State on submerged lands of a State; or

---

1. Editors' note: *See supra* at 23 n.1.

2. Editors' note: "Section 801 of Public Law 94-241" probably means section 801 of the Covenant to Establish a Commonwealth of the Northern Mariana Islands in Political Union with the United States of America, as contained in Pub. L. 94-241, §1, 90 Stat. 273 (1976), which is set out as a note under 48 U.S.C. §1801.

(3) on submerged lands of a State and is included in or determined eligible for inclusion in the National Register.

(b) [**Notice of shipwreck location; eligibility determination for inclusion in National Register of Historic Places**] The public shall be given adequate notice of the location of any shipwreck to which title is asserted under this section. The Secretary of the Interior, after consultation with the appropriate State Historic Preservation Officer, shall make a written determination that an abandoned shipwreck meets the criteria for eligibility for inclusion in the National Register of Historic Places under clause (a)(3).

(c) **Transfer of Title to States.** The title of the United States to any abandoned shipwreck asserted under subsection (a) of this section is transferred to the State in or on whose submerged lands the shipwreck is located.

(d) **Exception.** Any abandoned shipwreck in or on the public lands of the United States is the property of the United States Government. Any abandoned shipwreck in or on any Indian lands is the property of the Indian tribe owning such lands.

* * *

Abandoned Shipwreck Act § 7, 43 U.S.C. § 2106. Relationship to other laws.

(a) **Law of Salvage and the Law of Finds.** The law of salvage and the law of finds shall not apply to abandoned shipwrecks to which section 6 of this Act [43 U.S.C. § 2105] applies.

(b) **Laws of the United States.** This Act shall not change the laws of the United States relating to shipwrecks, other than those to which this Act applies.

(c) **Effective Date.** This Act shall not affect any legal proceeding brought prior to the date of enactment of this Act [April 28, 1988].

Federal Employers' Liability Act

Congress enacted the Federal Employers' Liability Act ("FELA"), 45 U.S.C. §§ 51–60, in 1908, 35 Stat. 65, after an earlier attempt had been held unconstitutional. The Act has since been amended on a few occasions. See, e.g., Federal Employers' Liability Act of 1939, 53 Stat. 1404, Federal Employers' Liability Act of 1910, 36 Stat. 291. Selected provisions of the Act, as amended, are reproduced here.

FELA § 1, 45 U.S.C. § 51. [Liability of common carriers by railroad, in interstate or foreign commerce, for injuries to employees from negligence; employee defined]

Every common carrier by railroad while engaging in commerce between any of the several States or Territories, or between any of the States and Territories, or between the District of Columbia and any of the States or Territories, or between the District of Columbia or any of the States or Territories and any foreign nation or nations, shall be liable in damages to any person suffering injury while he is employed by such carrier in such commerce, or, in case of the death of such employee, to his or her personal representative, for the benefit of the surviving widow or husband and children of such employee; and, if none, then of such employee's parents; and, if none, then of the next of kin dependent upon such employee, for such injury or death resulting in whole or in part from the negligence of any of the officers, agents, or employees of such carrier, or by reason of any defect or insufficiency, due to its negligence, in its cars, engines, appliances, machinery, track, roadbed, works, boats, wharves, or other equipment.

Any employee of a carrier, any part of whose duties as such employee shall be the furtherance of interstate or foreign commerce; or shall, in any way directly or closely and substantially, affect such commerce as above set forth shall, for the purposes of this Act, be considered as being employed by such carrier in such commerce and shall be considered as entitled to the benefits of [this Act], as the same has been or may hereafter be amended.

FELA § 3, 45 U.S.C. § 53. [Contributory negligence; diminution of damages]

In all actions hereafter brought against any such common carrier by railroad under or by virtue of any of the provisions of this Act to recover damages for personal injuries to an employee, or where such injuries have resulted in his death, the fact that the employee may have been guilty of contributory negligence shall not bar a recovery, but the damages shall be diminished by the jury in proportion to the amount of negligence attributable to such employee: *Provided*, That no such employee who may be injured or killed shall be held to have been guilty of contributory negligence in any case where the violation by such common carrier of any statute enacted for the safety of employees contributed to the injury or death of such employee.

FELA § 4, 45 U.S.C. § 54. [Assumption of risks of employment]

In any action brought against any common carrier under or by virtue of any of the provisions of this Act to recover damages for injuries to, or the death of, any of its employees, such employee shall not be held to have assumed the risks of his employment in any case where such injury or death resulted in whole or in part from the negligence of any of the officers, agents, or employees of such carrier; and no employee shall be held to have assumed the risks of his employment in any case where the violation by such common carrier of any statute enacted for the safety of employees contributed to the injury or death of such employee.

FELA § 5, 45 U.S.C. § 55. [Contract, rule, regulation, or device exempting from liability; set-off]

Any contract, rule, regulation, or device whatsoever, the purpose or intent of which shall be to enable any common carrier to exempt itself from any liability created by this Act, shall to that extent be void: *Provided,* That in any action brought against any such common carrier under or by virtue of any of the provisions of this Act, such common carrier may set off therein any sum it has contributed or paid to any insurance, relief benefit, or indemnity that may have been paid to the injured employee or the person entitled thereto on account of the injury or death for which said action was brought.

FELA § 6, 45 U.S.C. § 56. [Actions; limitations; concurrent jurisdiction of courts]

No action shall be maintained under this Act unless commenced within three years from the day the cause of action accrued.

Under this Act an action may be brought in a district court of the United States, in the district of the residence of the defendant, or in which the cause of action arose, or in which the defendant shall be doing business at the time of commencing such action. The jurisdiction of the courts of the United States under this Act shall be concurrent with that of the courts of the several States.

FELA § 9, 45 U.S.C. § 59. [Survival of right of action of person injured]

Any right of action given by this Act to a person suffering injury shall survive to his or her personal representative, for the benefit of the surviving widow or husband and children of such employee, and, if none, then of such employee's parents; and, if none, then of the next of kin dependent upon such employee, but in such cases there shall be only one recovery for the same injury.

The Recodification of Title 46

For much of the twentieth century, various government agencies attempted to update and codify U.S. shipping laws. In 1983, Congress finally took the first step in the process of revising title 46 of the United States Code and enacting it into positive law. In Public Law 98-89, 97 Stat. 509, Congress enacted subtitle II of title 46. As part of this recodification process, Congress moved the unrevised provisions of the old title 46 into an appendix in which the former section numbers were retained. Thus the Jones Act, which had been codified at 46 U.S.C. §688, found a new home at 46 U.S.C. app. §688. See infra at 34. These unrevised provisions of the old title 46 remained in the appendix until they were eventually recodified themselves.

Although revision and recodification of title 46 did not proceed as quickly as Congress had originally intended, the process did continue. In 1988, for example, the Federal Maritime Lien Act and the Ship Mortgage Act were recodified as 46 U.S.C. §§31301–43, and these provisions were enacted into positive law. 102 Stat. 4735. (Selected provisions are reproduced infra at 61.)

The recodification process was finally completed (subject to a final "clean-up" bill) in 2006, thus putting an end to the temporary "appendix." See Pub. L. No. 109-304, 120 Stat. 1485. The completion of the process was so recent, however, that courts continue to cite the old provisions that have been superseded. In any event, most of the cases included in the casebook were decided before the completion of the recodification process, and thus the opinions cite to the prior version of the law. As a matter of convenience, therefore, the prior versions are included in this supplement after each statute that was recodified in 2006. Having access to these prior versions may also help in understanding the current law because the recodification was not intended to result in any substantive change.

The first two provisions here were enacted into positive law in the 1983 Partial Revision of Title 46, which focused on maritime safety issues. These sections were based on prior statutory provisions, some of which dated from the nineteenth century. Section 2304 was amended in 2006 to add §2304(a)(2).

The third provision here was enacted into positive law in the 2006 recodification. Its predecessor statute, 46 U.S.C. app. §763a, dates from 1980, when Congress repealed the two-year statute of limitations previously contained in section 3 of the Death on the High Seas Act (DOHSA), which had until then been codified at 46 U.S.C. §763, and enacted a broader three-year statute of limitations. The new provision was not technically part of DOHSA, but it was codified with DOHSA for 26 years. As part of the 2006 recodification, it was finally separated from DOHSA and codified as part of the chapter entitled "General Liability Provisions."

46 U.S.C. §2303. Duties related to marine casualty assistance and information

(a) The master or individual in charge of a vessel involved in a marine casualty shall—

(1) render necessary assistance to each individual affected to save that affected individual from danger caused by the marine casualty, so far as the master or individual in charge can do so without serious danger to the master's or individual's vessel or to individuals on board; and

(2) give the master's or individual's name and address and identification of the vessel to the master or individual in charge of any other vessel involved in the casualty, to any individual injured, and to the owner of any property damaged.

(b) An individual violating this section or a regulation prescribed under this section shall be fined not more than $1,000 or imprisoned for not more than 2 years. The vessel also is liable in rem to the United States Government for the fine.

(c) An individual complying with subsection (a) of this section or gratuitously and in good faith rendering assistance at the scene of a marine casualty without objection by an individual assisted, is not liable for damages as a result of rendering assistance or for an act or omission in providing or arranging salvage, towage, medical treatment, or other assistance when the individual acts as an ordinary, reasonable, and prudent individual would have acted under the circumstances.

46 U.S.C. § 2304. Duty to provide assistance at sea

(a) (1) A master or individual in charge of a vessel shall render assistance to any individual found at sea in danger of being lost, so far as the master or individual in charge can do so without serious danger to the master's or individual's vessel or individuals on board.

(2) Paragraph (1) does not apply to a vessel of war or a vessel owned by the United States Government appropriated only to a public service.

(b) A master or individual violating this section shall be fined not more than $1,000, imprisoned for not more than 2 years, or both.

46 U.S.C. § 30106. Time limit on bringing maritime action for personal injury or death

Except as otherwise provided by law, a civil action for damages for personal injury or death arising out of a maritime tort must be brought within 3 years after the cause of action arose.

The Law Prior to the 2006 Recodification

Immediately prior to the 2006 recodification of Title 46, the predecessor of section 30106 was codified in the middle of DOHSA as 46 U.S.C. app. § 763a.

46 U.S.C. app. § 763a (2000). [Limitations]

Unless otherwise specified by law, a suit for recovery of damages for personal injury or death, or both, arising out of a maritime tort, shall not be maintained unless commenced within three years from the date the cause of action accrued.

Admiralty Extension Act

Congress originally enacted the Admiralty Extension Act, now codified at 46 U.S.C. §30101, in 1948. 62 Stat. 496. There is no official short title for the Act, and thus it is often cited by different names, such as the "Extension of Admiralty Jurisdiction Act" or the "Admiralty Jurisdiction Extension Act." The current language was enacted as part of the 2006 recodification of Title 46. See supra at 29.

§30101. Extension of jurisdiction to cases of damage or injury on land

(a) IN GENERAL—The admiralty and maritime jurisdiction of the United States extends to and includes cases of injury or damage, to person or property, caused by a vessel on navigable waters, even though the injury or damage is done or consummated on land.

(b) PROCEDURE—A civil action in a case under subsection (a) may be brought in rem or in personam according to the principles of law and the rules of practice applicable in cases where the injury or damage has been done and consummated on navigable waters.

(c) ACTIONS AGAINST UNITED STATES—

(1) EXCLUSIVE REMEDY—In a civil action against the United States for injury or damage done or consummated on land by a vessel on navigable waters, chapter 309 or 311 of this title, as appropriate, provides the exclusive remedy.

(2) ADMINISTRATIVE CLAIM—A civil action described in paragraph (1) may not be brought until the expiration of the 6-month period after the claim has been presented in writing to the agency owning or operating the vessel causing the injury or damage.

The Law Prior to the 2006 Recodification

Immediately prior to the 2006 recodification of Title 46, the Admiralty Extension Act was included in the appendix to Title 46. See supra at 29.

46 U.S.C. app. §740 (2000). Extension of admiralty and maritime jurisdiction; libel in rem or in personam; exclusive remedy; waiting period

The admiralty and maritime jurisdiction of the United States shall extend to and include all cases of damage or injury, to person or property, caused by a vessel on navigable water, notwithstanding that such damage or injury be done or consummated on land.

In any such case suit may be brought in rem or in personam according to the principles of law and the rules of practice obtaining in cases where the injury or damage has been done and consummated on navigable water: *Provided*, That as to any suit against the United States for damage or injury done or consummated on land by a vessel on navigable waters, the Public Vessels Act [46 U.S.C. §§31101–13 (previously codified at 46 U.S.C. app. §§781–790), *infra* at 57] or Suits in Admiralty Act [46 U.S.C. §§30901–18 (previously codified at 46 U.S.C. app. §§741–752), *infra* at 53], as appropriate, shall constitute the exclusive remedy for all causes of action arising after [June 19, 1948], and for all causes of action where suit has not been hitherto filed under the Federal Tort Claims Act [*supra* at 11]: *Provided further*, That no suit shall be filed against the United States until there shall have expired a period of six months after the claim has been presented in writing to the Federal agency owning or operating the vessel causing the injury or damage.

Jones Act

Congress enacted the original Jones Act, which is now 46 U.S.C. § 30104, in 1920. 41 Stat. 1007. The original language was codified for many years as 46 U.S.C. § 688, then as 46 U.S.C. § 688(a), and finally (until the 2006 recodification of Title 46) as 46 U.S.C. app. § 688(a). Congress amended the Act in 1982 to add what is now 46 U.S.C. § 30105. 96 Stat. 1955. This 1982 addition was first codified as 46 U.S.C. § 688(b) and then as 46 U.S.C. app. § 688(b).

The current language of the statute was enacted as part of the 2006 recodification of Title 46. See supra at 29. The 2006 recodification also included a § 30104(b), titled "venue," which provided that "[a]n action under this section shall be brought in the judicial district in which the employer resides or the employer's principal office is located." Although that provision closely tracked the final sentence of the original 1920 Act, it did not reflect judicial practice (which had limited the Jones Act venue rule to law-side actions while following admiralty and state venue rules for Jones Act cases in admiralty or state courts). The new § 30104(b) was accordingly deleted by Public Law 110-181, Div. C, Title XXXV, § 3521(b), 122 Stat. 596 (2008). The deletion was declared to "be effective as if included in the enactment of Public Law 109-304 [the 2006 recodification]."

§ 30104. Personal injury to or death of seamen

A seaman injured in the course of employment or, if the seaman dies from the injury, the personal representative of the seaman may elect to bring a civil action at law, with the right of trial by jury, against the employer. Laws of the United States regulating recovery for personal injury to, or death of, a railway employee[1] apply to an action under this section.

§ 30105. Restriction on recovery by non-citizens and non-resident aliens for incidents in waters of other countries

(a) Definition — In this section, the term "continental shelf" has the meaning given that term in article I of the 1958 Convention on the Continental Shelf.[2]

(b) Restriction — Except as provided in subsection (c), a civil action for maintenance and cure or for damages for personal injury or death may not be brought under a maritime law of the United States if—

(1) the individual suffering the injury or death was not a citizen or permanent resident alien of the United States at the time of the incident giving rise to the action;

(2) the incident occurred in the territorial waters or waters overlaying the continental shelf of a country other than the United States; and

(3) the individual suffering the injury or death was employed at the time of the incident by a person engaged in the exploration, development, or production of offshore mineral or energy resources, including drilling, mapping, surveying, diving, pipelaying, maintaining, repairing, constructing, or transporting supplies, equipment,

---

1. Editors' note: The reference is to the Federal Employers Liability Act, as amended ("FELA"), 45 U.S.C. §§ 51–60, *supra* at 27.

2. Editors' note: The reference is to the Geneva Convention on the Continental Shelf, April 29, 1958, art. 1, 499 U.N.T.S. 311, 312, 15 U.S.T. 471, 473, T.I.A.S. 5578, which entered into force for the United States on June 10, 1964. Article 1 provides that "the term 'continental shelf' is used as referring (*a*) to the seabed and subsoil of the submarine areas adjacent to the coast but outside the area of the territorial sea, to a depth of 200 metres or, beyond that limit, to where the depth of the superjacent waters admits of the exploitation of the natural resources of the said areas; (*b*) to the seabed and subsoil of similar submarine areas adjacent to the coasts of islands."

or personnel, but not including transporting those resources by a vessel constructed or adapted primarily to carry oil in bulk in the cargo spaces.

(c) NONAPPLICATION—Subsection (b) does not apply if the individual bringing the action establishes that a remedy is not available under the laws of—

(1) the country asserting jurisdiction over the area in which the incident occurred; or

(2) the country in which the individual suffering the injury or death maintained citizenship or residency at the time of the incident.

The Law Prior to the 2006 Recodification

Immediately prior to the 2006 recodification of Title 46, the Jones Act was included in the appendix to Title 46. See supra at 29.

46 U.S.C. app. §688 (2000). Recovery for injury to or death of seaman

(a) Any seaman who shall suffer personal injury in the course of his employment may, at his election, maintain an action for damages at law, with the right of trial by jury, and in such action all statutes of the United States modifying or extending the common-law right or remedy in cases of personal injury to railway employees[1] shall apply; and in case of the death of any seaman as a result of any such personal injury the personal representative of such seaman may maintain an action for damages at law with the right of trial by jury, and in such action all statutes of the United States conferring or regulating the right of action for death in the case of railway employees shall be applicable. Jurisdiction in such actions shall be under the court of the district in which the defendant employer resides or in which his principal office is located.

(b)(1) No action may be maintained under subsection (a) of this section or under any other maritime law of the United States for maintenance and cure or for damages for the injury or death of a person who was not a citizen or permanent resident alien of the United States at the time of the incident giving rise to the action if the incident occurred—

(A) while that person was in the employ of an enterprise engaged in the exploration, development, or production of offshore mineral or energy resources—including but not limited to drilling, mapping, surveying, diving, pipelaying, maintaining, repairing, constructing, or transporting supplies, equipment or personnel, but not including transporting those resources by [a] vessel constructed or adapted primarily to carry oil in bulk in the cargo spaces; and

(B) in the territorial waters or waters overlaying the continental shelf of a nation other than the United States, its territories, or possessions. As used in this paragraph, the term "continental shelf" has the meaning stated in article I of the 1958 Convention on the Continental Shelf.[2]

(2) The provisions of paragraph (1) of this subsection shall not be applicable if the person bringing the action establishes that no remedy was available to that person—

(A) under the laws of the nation asserting jurisdiction over the area in which the incident occurred; or

---

1. Editors' note: The reference is to the Federal Employers Liability Act, as amended ("FELA"), 45 U.S.C. §§51–60, *supra* at 27.

2. Editors' note: The reference is to the Geneva Convention on the Continental Shelf, April 29, 1958, art. 1, 499 U.N.T.S. 311, 312, 15 U.S.T. 471, 473, T.I.A.S. 5578. *See supra* at 33 n.2.

(B) under the laws of the nation in which, at the time of the incident, the person for whose injury or death a remedy is sought maintained citizenship or residency.

Death on the High Seas Act

Congress originally enacted the Death on the High Seas Act ("DOHSA"), now codified at 46 U.S.C. §§ 30301–08, in 1920. 41 Stat. 537. In 1980, Congress repealed the two-year statute of limitations in DOHSA § 3, previously codified at 46 U.S.C. § 763, and enacted a broader three-year statute of limitations now codified at 46 U.S.C. § 30106 (reprinted supra at 30). 94 Stat. 1525. Congress amended the Act again in 2000 to expand the remedies available following commercial aviation accidents. The current language was enacted as chapter 303 of Title 46 as part of the 2006 recodification. See supra at 29.

§ 30301. Short title

This chapter may be cited as the "Death on the High Seas Act".

§ 30302. Cause of action

When the death of an individual is caused by wrongful act, neglect, or default occurring on the high seas beyond 3 nautical miles from the shore of the United States, the personal representative of the decedent may bring a civil action in admiralty against the person or vessel responsible. The action shall be for the exclusive benefit of the decedent's spouse, parent, child, or dependent relative.

§ 30303. Amount and apportionment of recovery

The recovery in an action under this chapter shall be a fair compensation for the pecuniary loss sustained by the individuals for whose benefit the action is brought. The court shall apportion the recovery among those individuals in proportion to the loss each has sustained.

§ 30304. Contributory negligence

In an action under this chapter, contributory negligence of the decedent is not a bar to recovery. The court shall consider the degree of negligence of the decedent and reduce the recovery accordingly.

§ 30305. Death of plaintiff in pending action

If a civil action in admiralty is pending in a court of the United States to recover for personal injury caused by wrongful act, neglect, or default described in section 30302 of this title, and the individual dies during the action as a result of the wrongful act, neglect, or default, the personal representative of the decedent may be substituted as the plaintiff and the action may proceed under this chapter for the recovery authorized by this chapter.

§ 30306. Foreign cause of action

When a cause of action exists under the law of a foreign country for death by wrongful act, neglect, or default on the high seas, a civil action in admiralty may be brought in a court of the United States based on the foreign cause of action, without abatement of the amount for which recovery is authorized.

§ 30307. Commercial aviation accidents

(a) DEFINITION—In this section, the term "nonpecuniary damages" means damages for loss of care, comfort, and companionship.

(b) BEYOND 12 NAUTICAL MILES—In an action under this chapter, if the death resulted from a commercial aviation accident occurring on the high seas beyond 12 nautical miles from the shore of the United States, additional compensation is recoverable for nonpecuniary damages, but punitive damages are not recoverable.

(c) WITHIN 12 NAUTICAL MILES—This chapter does not apply if the death resulted from a commercial aviation accident occurring on the high seas 12 nautical miles or less from the shore of the United States.

§ 30308. Nonapplication

(a) STATE LAW—This chapter does not affect the law of a State regulating the right to recover for death.

(b) INTERNAL WATERS—This chapter does not apply to the Great Lakes or waters within the territorial limits of a State.

The Law Prior to the 2006 Recodification

Immediately prior to the 2006 recodification of Title 46, DOHSA was included in the appendix to Title 46. See supra at 29.

DOHSA § 1, 46 U.S.C. app. § 761 (2000). [Right of action; where and by whom brought]

(a) Subject to subsection (b), whenever the death of a person shall be caused by wrongful act, neglect, or default occurring on the high seas beyond a marine league from the shore of any State, or the District of Columbia, or the Territories or dependencies of the United States, the personal representative of the decedent may maintain a suit for damages in the district courts of the United States, in admiralty, for the exclusive benefit of the decedent's wife, husband, parent, child, or dependent relative against the vessel, person, or corporation which would have been liable if death had not ensued.

(b) In the case of a commercial aviation accident, whenever the death of a person shall be caused by wrongful act, neglect, or default occurring on the high seas 12 nautical miles or closer to the shore of any State, or the District of Columbia, or the Territories or dependencies of the United States, this Act shall not apply and the rules applicable under Federal, State, and other appropriate law shall apply.

DOHSA § 2, 46 U.S.C. app. § 762 (2000). [Amount and apportionment of recovery]

(a) The recovery in such suit shall be a fair and just compensation for the pecuniary loss sustained by the persons for whose benefit the suit is brought and shall be apportioned among them by the court in proportion to the loss they may severally have suffered by reason of the death of the person by whose representative the suit is brought.

(b)(1) If the death resulted from a commercial aviation accident occurring on the high seas beyond 12 nautical miles from the shore of any State, or the District of Columbia, or the Territories or dependencies of the United States, additional compensation for nonpecuniary damages for wrongful death of a decedent is recoverable. Punitive damages are not recoverable.

(2) In this subsection, the term "nonpecuniary damages" means damages for loss of care, comfort, and companionship.

DOHSA § 4, 46 U.S.C. app. § 764 (2000). [Rights of action given by laws of foreign countries]

Whenever a right of action is granted by the law of any foreign State on account of death by wrongful act, neglect, or default occurring upon the high seas, such right may be maintained in an appropriate action in admiralty in the courts of the United States without abatement in respect to the amount for which recovery is authorized, any statute of the United States to the contrary notwithstanding.

DOHSA §5, 46 U.S.C. app. §765 (2000). [Death of plaintiff pending action]

If a person die[s] as the result of such wrongful act, neglect, or default as is mentioned in section 1 [former 46 U.S.C. app. §761] during the pendency in a court of admiralty of the United States of a suit to recover damages for personal injuries in respect of such act, neglect, or default, the personal representative of the decedent may be substituted as a party and the suit may proceed as a suit under this Act for the recovery of the compensation provided in section 2 [former 46 U.S.C. app. §762].

DOHSA §6, 46 U.S.C. app. §766 (2000). [Contributory negligence]

In suits under this Act the fact that the decedent has been guilty of contributory negligence shall not bar recovery, but the court shall take into consideration the degree of negligence attributable to the decedent and reduce the recovery accordingly.

DOHSA §7, 46 U.S.C. app. §767 (2000). [Exceptions from operation of chapter]

The provisions of any State statute giving or regulating rights of action or remedies for death shall not be affected by this Act. Nor shall this Act apply to the Great Lakes or to any waters within the territorial limits of any State, or to any navigable waters in the Panama Canal Zone.

Limitation Act

The Limitation Act, also known by other names (such as the Limited Liability Act), was originally passed in 1851. 9 Stat. 635. It was codified, as amended, in the Revised Statutes, which were enacted as positive law in 1874. 18 Stat. 831–833. The Limitation Act was again codified in the mid-1920s, unofficially this time, as part of Title 46 of the United States Code. The current language was enacted as chapter 305 of Title 46 as part of the 2006 recodification. See supra at 29.

§ 30501. Definition

In this chapter, the term "owner" includes a charterer that mans, supplies, and navigates a vessel at the charterer's own expense or by the charterer's own procurement.

§ 30502. Application

Except as otherwise provided, this chapter (except section 30503) applies to seagoing vessels and vessels used on lakes or rivers or in inland navigation, including canal boats, barges, and lighters.

§ 30503. Declaration of nature and value of goods

(a) IN GENERAL—If a shipper of an item named in subsection (b), contained in a parcel, package, or trunk, loads the item as freight or baggage on a vessel, without at the time of loading giving to the person receiving the item a written notice of the true character and value of the item and having that information entered on the bill of lading, the owner and master of the vessel are not liable as carriers. The owner and master are not liable beyond the value entered on the bill of lading.

(b) ITEMS—The items referred to in subsection (a) are precious metals, gold or silver plated articles, precious stones, jewelry, trinkets, watches, clocks, glass, china, coins, bills, securities, printings, engravings, pictures, stamps, maps, papers, silks, furs, lace, and similar items of high value and small size.

§ 30504. Loss by fire

The owner of a vessel is not liable for loss or damage to merchandise on the vessel caused by a fire on the vessel unless the fire resulted from the design or neglect of the owner.

§ 30505. General limit of liability

(a) IN GENERAL—Except as provided in section 30506 of this title, the liability of the owner of a vessel for any claim, debt, or liability described in subsection (b) shall not exceed the value of the vessel and pending freight. If the vessel has more than one owner, the proportionate share of the liability of any one owner shall not exceed that owner's proportionate interest in the vessel and pending freight.

(b) CLAIMS SUBJECT TO LIMITATION—Unless otherwise excluded by law, claims, debts, and liabilities subject to limitation under subsection (a) are those arising from any embezzlement, loss, or destruction of any property, goods, or merchandise shipped or put on board the vessel, any loss, damage, or injury by collision, or any act, matter, or thing, loss, damage, or forfeiture, done, occasioned, or incurred, without the privity or knowledge of the owner.

(c) WAGES—Subsection (a) does not apply to a claim for wages.

§ 30506. Limit of liability for personal injury or death

(a) APPLICATION—This section applies only to seagoing vessels, but does not apply to pleasure yachts, tugs, towboats, towing vessels, tank vessels, fishing vessels, fish tender vessels, canal boats, scows, car floats, barges, lighters, or nondescript vessels.

(b) MINIMUM LIABILITY—If the amount of the vessel owner's liability determined under section 30505 of this title is insufficient to pay all losses in full, and the portion available to pay claims for personal injury or death is less than $420 times the tonnage of the vessel, that portion shall be increased to $420 times the tonnage of the vessel. That portion may be used only to pay claims for personal injury or death.

(c) CALCULATION OF TONNAGE—Under subsection (b), the tonnage of a self-propelled vessel is the gross tonnage without deduction for engine room, and the tonnage of a sailing vessel is the tonnage for documentation. However, space for the use of seamen is excluded.

(d) CLAIMS ARISING ON DISTINCT OCCASIONS—Separate limits of liability apply to claims for personal injury or death arising on distinct occasions.

(e) PRIVITY OR KNOWLEDGE—In a claim for personal injury or death, the privity or knowledge of the master or the owner's superintendent or managing agent, at or before the beginning of each voyage, is imputed to the owner.

§ 30507. Apportionment of losses

If the amounts determined under sections 30505 and 30506 of this title are insufficient to pay all claims—

(1) all claimants shall be paid in proportion to their respective losses out of the amount determined under section 30505 of this title; and

(2) personal injury and death claimants, if any, shall be paid an additional amount in proportion to their respective losses out of the additional amount determined under section 30506(b) of this title.

§ 30508. Provisions requiring notice of claim or limiting time for bringing action

(a) APPLICATION—This section applies only to seagoing vessels, but does not apply to pleasure yachts, tugs, towboats, towing vessels, tank vessels, fishing vessels, fish tender vessels, canal boats, scows, car floats, barges, lighters, or nondescript vessels.

(b) MINIMUM TIME LIMITS—The owner, master, manager, or agent of a vessel transporting passengers or property between ports in the United States, or between a port in the United States and a port in a foreign country, may not limit by regulation, contract, or otherwise the period for—

(1) giving notice of, or filing a claim for, personal injury or death to less than 6 months after the date of the injury or death; or

(2) bringing a civil action for personal injury or death to less than one year after the date of the injury or death.

(c) EFFECT OF FAILURE TO GIVE NOTICE—When notice of a claim for personal injury or death is required by a contract, the failure to give the notice is not a bar to recovery if—

(1) the court finds that the owner, master, or agent of the vessel had knowledge of the injury or death and the owner has not been prejudiced by the failure;

(2) the court finds there was a satisfactory reason why the notice could not have been given; or

(3) the owner of the vessel fails to object to the failure to give the notice.

(d) Tolling of Period to Give Notice—If a claimant is a minor or mental incompetent, or if a claim is for wrongful death, any period provided by a contract for giving notice of the claim is tolled until the earlier of—

(1) the date a legal representative is appointed for the minor, incompetent, or decedent's estate; or

(2) 3 years after the injury or death.

§ 30509. Provisions limiting liability for personal injury or death

(a) Prohibition—

(1) In General—The owner, master, manager, or agent of a vessel transporting passengers between ports in the United States, or between a port in the United States and a port in a foreign country, may not include in a regulation or contract a provision limiting—

(A) the liability of the owner, master, or agent for personal injury or death caused by the negligence or fault of the owner or the owner's employees or agents; or

(B) the right of a claimant for personal injury or death to a trial by court of competent jurisdiction.

(2) Voidness—A provision described in paragraph (1) is void.

(b) Emotional Distress, Mental Suffering, and Psychological Injury—

(1) In General—Subsection (a) does not prohibit a provision in a contract or in ticket conditions of carriage with a passenger that relieves an owner, master, manager, agent, operator, or crewmember of a vessel from liability for infliction of emotional distress, mental suffering, or psychological injury so long as the provision does not limit such liability when the emotional distress, mental suffering, or psychological injury is—

(A) the result of physical injury to the claimant caused by the negligence or fault of a crewmember or the owner, master, manager, agent, or operator;

(B) the result of the claimant having been at actual risk of physical injury, and the risk was caused by the negligence or fault of a crewmember or the owner, master, manager, agent, or operator; or

(C) intentionally inflicted by a crewmember or the owner, master, manager, agent, or operator.

(2) Sexual Offenses—This subsection does not limit the liability of a crewmember or the owner, master, manager, agent, or operator of a vessel in a case involving sexual harassment, sexual assault, or rape.

§ 30510. Vicarious liability for medical malpractice with regard to crew

In a civil action by any person in which the owner or operator of a vessel or employer of a crewmember is claimed to have vicarious liability for medical malpractice with regard to a crewmember occurring at a shoreside facility, and to the extent the damages resulted from the conduct of any shoreside doctor, hospital, medical facility, or other health care provider, the owner, operator, or employer is entitled to rely on any statutory limitations of liability applicable to the doctor, hospital, medical facility, or other health care provider in the State of the United States in which the shoreside medical care was provided.

§ 30511. Action by owner for limitation

(a) IN GENERAL—The owner of a vessel may bring a civil action in a district court of the United States for limitation of liability under this chapter. The action must be brought within 6 months after a claimant gives the owner written notice of a claim.

(b) CREATION OF FUND—When the action is brought, the owner (at the owner's option) shall—

(1) deposit with the court, for the benefit of claimants—

(A) an amount equal to the value of the owner's interest in the vessel and pending freight, or approved security; and

(B) an amount, or approved security, that the court may fix from time to time as necessary to carry out this chapter; or

(2) transfer to a trustee appointed by the court, for the benefit of claimants—

(A) the owner's interest in the vessel and pending freight; and

(B) an amount, or approved security, that the court may fix from time to time as necessary to carry out this chapter.

(c) CESSATION OF OTHER ACTIONS—When an action has been brought under this section and the owner has complied with subsection (b), all claims and proceedings against the owner related to the matter in question shall cease.

§ 30512. Liability as master, officer, or seaman not affected

This chapter does not affect the liability of an individual as a master, officer, or seaman, even though the individual is also an owner of the vessel.

The Law Prior to the 2006 Recodification

Immediately prior to the 2006 recodification of Title 46, the Limitation Act was included in the appendix to Title 46. See supra at 29. In reprinting the pre-2006 provisions here, we have included the Revised Statutes citation (which had been the authoritative citation prior to the 2006 recodification), a parenthetical reference to the section of the original 1851 Limitation Act on which the provision was based (often with substantial amendment), and the more convenient United States Code citation that was commonly used.

Revised Statutes § 4281 (Limitation Act § 2), 46 U.S.C. app. § 181 (2000). [Liability of masters as carriers]

If any shipper of platina, gold, gold dust, silver, bullion, or other precious metals, coins, jewelry, bills of any bank or public body, diamonds, or other precious stones, or any gold or silver in a manufactured or unmanufactured state, watches, clocks, or timepieces of any description, trinkets, orders, notes, or securities for payment of money, stamps, maps, writings, title deeds, printings, engravings, pictures, gold or silver plate or plated articles, glass, china, silks in a manufactured or unmanufactured state, and whether wrought up or not wrought up with any other material, furs, or lace, or any of them, contained in any parcel, or package, or trunk, shall lade the same as freight or baggage, on any vessel, without at the time of such lading giving to the master, clerk, agent, or owner of such vessel receiving the same a written notice of the true character and value thereof, and having the same entered on the bill of lading therefor, the master and owner of such vessel shall not be liable as carriers thereof in any form or manner; nor shall any such master or owner be liable for any such goods beyond the value and according to the character thereof so notified and entered.

Revised Statutes § 4282 (Limitation Act § 1), 46 U.S.C. app. § 182 (2000). [Loss by fire (the "Fire Statute")]

No owner of any vessel shall be liable to answer for or make good to any person any loss or damage, which may happen to any merchandise whatsoever, which shall be shipped, taken in, or put on board any such vessel, by reason or by means of any fire happening to or on board the vessel, unless such fire is caused by the design or neglect of such owner.

Revised Statutes § 4283 (Limitation Act § 3), 46 U.S.C. app. § 183 (2000). [Amount of liability]

(a) The liability of the owner of any vessel, whether American or foreign, for any embezzlement, loss, or destruction by any person of any property, goods, or merchandise shipped or put on board of such vessel, or for any loss, damage, or injury by collision, or for any act, matter, or thing, loss, damage, or forfeiture, done, occasioned, or incurred, without the privity or knowledge of such owner or owners, shall not, except in the cases provided for in subsection (b) of this section, exceed the amount or value of the interest of such owner in such vessel, and her freight then pending.

(b) In the case of any seagoing vessel, if the amount of the owner's liability as limited under subsection (a) of this section is insufficient to pay all losses in full, and the portion of such amount applicable to the payment of losses in respect of loss of life or bodily injury is less than $420 per ton of such vessel's tonnage, such portion shall be increased to an amount equal to $420 per ton, to be available only for the payment of losses in respect of loss of life or bodily injury. If such portion so increased is insufficient to pay such losses in full, they shall be paid therefrom in proportion to their respective amounts.

(c) For the purposes of this section the tonnage of a seagoing steam or motor vessel shall be her gross tonnage without deduction on account of engine room, and the tonnage of a seagoing sailing vessel shall be her registered tonnage: *Provided*, That there shall not be included in such tonnage any space occupied by seamen or apprentices and appropriated to their use.

(d) The owner of any such seagoing vessel shall be liable in respect of loss of life or bodily injury arising on distinct occasions to the same extent as if no other loss of life or bodily injury had arisen.

(e) In respect of loss of life or bodily injury the privity or knowledge of the master of a seagoing vessel or of the superintendent or managing agent of the owner thereof, at or prior to the commencement of each voyage, shall be deemed conclusively the privity or knowledge of the owner of such vessel.

(f) As used in subsections (b), (c), (d), and (e) of this section and in section 4283A [former 46 U.S.C. app. § 183b], the term "seagoing vessel" shall not include pleasure yachts, tugs, towboats, towing vessels, tank vessels, fishing vessels or their tenders, self-propelled lighters, nondescript self-propelled vessels, canal boats, scows, car floats, barges, lighters, or nondescript non-self-propelled vessels, even though the same may be seagoing vessels within the meaning of such term as used in section 4289 of this chapter [former 46 U.S.C. app. § 188], as amended.

(g) In a suit by any person in which the operator or owner of a vessel or employer of a crewmember is claimed to have vicarious liability for medical malpractice with regard to a crewmember occurring at a shoreside facility, and to the extent the damages resulted from the conduct of any shoreside doctor, hospital, medical facility, or other health care provider, such operator, owner, or employer shall be entitled to rely upon any and all statutory limitations of liability applicable to the doctor, hospital, medical facility, or other health care provider in the State of the United States in which the shoreside medical care was provided.

Revised Statutes § 4283A, 46 U.S.C. app. § 183b (2000). [Stipulations limiting time for filing claims and commencing suit]

(a) It shall be unlawful for the manager, agent, master, or owner of any sea-going vessel (other than tugs, barges, fishing vessels and their tenders) transporting passengers or merchandise or property from or between ports of the United States and foreign ports to provide by rule, contract, regulation, or otherwise a shorter period for giving notice of, or filing claims for loss of life or bodily injury, than six months, and for the institution of suits on such claims, than one year, such period for institution of suits to be computed from the day when the death or injury occurred.

* * *

Revised Statutes § 4283B, 46 U.S.C. app. § 183c (2000). [Stipulations limiting liability for negligence invalid; certain exceptions regarding infliction of emotional distress, etc.]

(a) It shall be unlawful for the manager, agent, master, or owner of any vessel transporting passengers between ports of the United States or between any such port and a foreign port to insert in any rule, regulation, contract, or agreement any provision or limitation (1) purporting, in the event of loss of life or bodily injury arising from the negligence or fault of such owner or his servants, to relieve such owner, master, or agent from liability, or from liability beyond any stipulated amount, for such loss or injury, or (2) purporting in such event to lessen, weaken, or avoid the right of any claimant to a trial by court of competent jurisdiction on the question of liability for such loss or injury, or the measure of damages therefor. All such provisions or limitations contained in any such rule, regulation, contract, or agreement are declared to be against public policy and shall be null and void and of no effect.

(b)(1) Subsection (a) of this section shall not prohibit provisions or limitations in contracts, agreements, or ticket conditions of carriage with passengers which relieve a crewmember, manager, agent, master, owner, or operator of a vessel from liability for infliction of emotional distress, mental suffering, or psychological injury so long as such provisions or limitations do not limit such liability if the emotional distress, mental suffering, or psychological injury was—

(A) the result of physical injury to the claimant caused by the negligence or fault of a crewmember or the manager, agent, master, owner, or operator;

(B) the result of the claimant having been at actual risk of physical injury, and such risk was caused by the negligence or fault of a crewmember or the manager, agent, master, owner, or operator; or

(C) intentionally inflicted by a crewmember or the manager, agent, master, owner, or operator.

(2) Nothing in this subsection is intended to limit the liability of a crewmember or the manager, agent, master, owner, or operator of a vessel in a case involving sexual harassment, sexual assault, or rape.

Revised Statutes § 4285 (Limitation Act § 4, second sentence), 46 U.S.C. app. § 185 (2000). [Petition for limitation of liability; deposit of value of interest in court; transfer of interest to trustee]

The vessel owner, within six months after a claimant shall have given to or filed with such owner written notice of claim, may petition a district court of the United States of competent jurisdiction for limitation of liability within the provisions of [former 46 U.S.C. app. §§ 181–195] and the owner (a) shall deposit with the court, for the benefit of claimants, a sum equal to the amount or value of the interest of such owner in the vessel and freight, or approved security therefor, and in addition such sums, or approved security therefor, as the court may from time to time fix as necessary to carry out the provisions of [former 46 U.S.C. app. § 183], or (b) at his option shall transfer, for the benefit of claimants, to a trustee to be appointed by the court his interest in the vessel and freight, together with such sums, or approved security therefor, as the court may from time to time fix as necessary to carry out the provisions of [former 46 U.S.C. app. § 183]. Upon compliance with the requirements of this section all claims and proceedings against the owner with respect to the matter in question shall cease.

Revised Statutes § 4286 (Limitation Act § 5), 46 U.S.C. app. § 186 (2000). [Charterer may be deemed owner]

The charterer of any vessel, in case he shall man, victual, and navigate such vessel at his own expense, or by his own procurement, shall be deemed the owner of such vessel within the meaning of the provisions of [title 48 of the Revised Statutes, §§ 4131–4305] relating to the limitation of the liability of the owners of vessels;[1] and such vessel, when so chartered, shall be liable in the same manner as if navigated by the owner thereof.

Revised Statutes § 4287 (Limitation Act § 6), 46 U.S.C. app. § 187 (2000). [Remedies reserved]

Nothing in [former 46 U.S.C. app. §§ 182, 183, 184, 185, and 186] shall be construed * * * to lessen or take away any responsibility to which any master or seamen of any vessel may by law be liable, notwithstanding such master or seaman may be an owner or part owner of the vessel.

Revised Statutes § 4289 (Limitation Act § 7, second paragraph), 46 U.S.C. app. § 188 (2000). [Limitation of liability of owners applied to all vessels]

Except as otherwise specifically provided therein, the provisions of [former 46 U.S.C. app. §§ 182, 183, 183b–187, 189] shall apply to all seagoing vessels, and also to all vessels used on lakes or rivers or in inland navigation, including canal boats, barges, and lighters.

Shipping Act of 1884, § 18, 23 Stat. 57, 46 U.S.C. app. § 189 (2000). [Limitation of liability of owners of vessels for debts]

The individual liability of a shipowner shall be limited to the proportion of any or all debts and liabilities that his individual share of the vessel bears to the whole; and the aggregate liabilities of all the owners of a vessel on account of the same shall not exceed the value of such vessels and freight pending: *Provided*, That this provision shall not * * * prevent any claimant from joining all the owners in one action; nor shall the same apply to wages due to persons employed by said shipowners.

---

1. Editors' note: The reference was presumably intended to be to those sections in the Revised Statutes that are derived from the Limitation Act, *i.e.*, Revised Statutes §§ 4281–4289.

Harter Act

Congress originally enacted the Harter Act in 1893. 27 Stat. 445. Although the Act was largely superseded in 1936 by the Carriage of Goods by Sea Act (COGSA), infra at 67, it has never been repealed and was not formally amended until the 2006 recodification (when the current language was enacted as chapter 307 of Title 46). See supra at 29.

§ 30701. Definition

In this chapter, the term "carrier" means the owner, manager, charterer, agent, or master of a vessel.

§ 30702. Application

(a) IN GENERAL—Except as otherwise provided, this chapter applies to a carrier engaged in the carriage of goods to or from any port in the United States.

(b) LIVE ANIMALS—Sections 30703 and 30704 of this title do not apply to the carriage of live animals.

§ 30703. Bills of lading

(a) ISSUANCE—On demand of a shipper, the carrier shall issue a bill of lading or shipping document.

(b) CONTENTS—The bill of lading or shipping document shall include a statement of—

(1) the marks necessary to identify the goods;

(2) the number of packages, or the quantity or weight, and whether it is carrier's or shipper's weight; and

(3) the apparent condition of the goods.

(c) PRIMA FACIE EVIDENCE OF RECEIPT—A bill of lading or shipping document issued under this section is prima facie evidence of receipt of the goods described.

§ 30704. Loading, stowage, custody, care, and delivery

A carrier may not insert in a bill of lading or shipping document a provision avoiding its liability for loss or damage arising from negligence or fault in loading, stowage, custody, care, or proper delivery. Any such provision is void.

§ 30705. Seaworthiness

(a) PROHIBITION—A carrier may not insert in a bill of lading or shipping document a provision lessening or avoiding its obligation to exercise due diligence to—

(1) make the vessel seaworthy; and

(2) properly man, equip, and supply the vessel.

(b) VOIDNESS—A provision described in subsection (a) is void.

§ 30706. Defenses

(a) DUE DILIGENCE—If a carrier has exercised due diligence to make the vessel in all respects seaworthy and to properly man, equip, and supply the vessel, the carrier and the vessel are not liable for loss or damage arising from an error in the navigation or management of the vessel.

(b) OTHER DEFENSES—A carrier and the vessel are not liable for loss or damage arising from—

(1) dangers of the sea or other navigable waters;

(2) acts of God;

(3) public enemies;

(4) seizure under legal process;

(5) inherent defect, quality, or vice of the goods;

(6) insufficiency of package;

(7) act or omission of the shipper or owner of the goods or their agent; or

(8) saving or attempting to save life or property at sea, including a deviation in rendering such a service.

§ 30707. Criminal penalty

(a) IN GENERAL—A carrier that violates this chapter shall be fined under title 18.

(b) LIEN—The amount of the fine and costs for the violation constitute a lien on the vessel engaged in the carriage. A civil action in rem to enforce the lien may be brought in the district court of the United States for any district in which the vessel is found.

(c) DISPOSITION OF FINE—Half of the fine shall go to the person injured by the violation and half to the United States Government.

The Law Prior to the 2006 Recodification

Immediately prior to the 2006 recodification of Title 46, the Harter Act was included in the appendix to Title 46. See supra at 29.

Harter Act § 1, 46 U.S.C. app. § 190 (2000). [Stipulations relieving from liability for negligence]

It shall not be lawful for the manager, agent, master, or owner of any vessel transporting merchandise or property from or between ports of the United States and foreign ports to insert in any bill of lading or shipping document any clause, covenant, or agreement whereby it, he, or they shall be relieved from liability for loss or damage arising from negligence, fault, or failure in proper loading, stowage, custody, care, or proper delivery of any and all lawful merchandise or property committed to its or their charge. Any and all words or clauses of such import inserted in bills of lading or shipping receipts shall be null and void and of no effect.

Harter Act § 2, 46 U.S.C. app. § 191 (2000). [Stipulations relieving from exercise of due diligence in equipping vessels]

It shall not be lawful for any vessel transporting merchandise or property from or between ports of the United States of America and foreign ports, her owner, master, agent, or manager, to insert in any bill of lading or shipping document any covenant or agreement whereby the obligations of the owner or owners of said vessel to exercise due diligence properly [to] equip, man, provision, and outfit said vessel, and to make said vessel seaworthy and capable of performing her intended voyage, or whereby the obligations of the master, officers, agents, or servants to carefully handle and stow her cargo and to care for and properly deliver same, shall in any wise be lessened, weakened, or avoided.

Harter Act § 3, 46 U.S.C. app. § 192 (2000). [Limitation of liability for errors of navigation, dangers of the sea and acts of God]

If the owner of any vessel transporting merchandise or property to or from any port in the United States of America shall exercise due diligence to make the said vessel in all respects seaworthy and properly manned, equipped, and supplied, neither the vessel, her owner or owners, agent, or charterers, shall become or be held responsible for damage or loss resulting from faults or errors in navigation or in the management of said vessel nor shall the vessel, her owner or owners, charterers, agent, or master be held liable for losses arising from dangers of the sea or other navigable waters, acts of God, or public enemies, or the inherent defect, quality, or vice of the thing carried, or from insufficiency of package, or seizure under legal process, or for loss resulting from any act or omission of the shipper or owner of the goods, his agent or representative, or from saving or attempting to save life or property at sea, or from any deviation in rendering such service.

Harter Act § 4, 46 U.S.C. app. § 193 (2000). [Bills of lading to be issued; contents]

It shall be the duty of the owner or owners, masters, or agents of any vessel transporting merchandise or property from or between ports of the United States and foreign ports to issue to shippers of any lawful merchandise a bill of lading, or shipping document, stating, among other things, the marks necessary for identification, number of packages, or quantity, stating whether it be carrier's or shipper's weight, and apparent order or condition of such merchandise or property delivered to and received by the owner, master, or agent of the vessel for transportation, and such document shall be prima facie evidence of the receipt of the merchandise therein described.

Harter Act § 5, 46 U.S.C. app. § 194 (2000). [Penalties; lien; recovery]

For a violation of any of the provisions of this act the agent, owner, or master of the vessel guilty of such violation, and who refuses to issue on demand the bill of lading herein provided for, shall be liable to a fine not exceeding two thousand dollars. The amount of the fine and costs for such violation shall be a lien upon the vessel, whose agent, owner, or master is guilty of such violation, and such vessel may be libeled therefor in any district court of the United States, within whose jurisdiction the vessel may be found. One-half of such penalty shall go to the party injured by such violation and the remainder to the Government of the United States.

Harter Act § 7, 46 U.S.C. app. § 195 (2000). [Certain provisions inapplicable to transportation of live animals]

Sections one and four of this act [previously codified at 46 U.S.C. app. §§ 190, 193] shall not apply to the transportation of live animals.

Harter Act § 6, 46 U.S.C. app. § 196 (2000). [Certain laws unaffected]

This act shall not be held to modify or repeal [Revised Statutes §§ 4281–83, previously codified at 46 U.S.C. app. §§ 181–183], or any other statute defining the liability of vessels, their owners, or representatives.

Suits in Admiralty Act

Congress originally enacted the Suits in Admiralty Act, now codified at 46 U.S.C. §§ 30901–18, in 1920. 41 Stat. 525. Over the rest of the century, it was amended several times in relatively minor ways. The current language was enacted as chapter 309 of Title 46 as part of the 2006 recodification. See supra at 29.

§ 30901. Short title

This chapter may be cited as the "Suits in Admiralty Act."

§ 30902. Definition

In this chapter, the term "federally-owned corporation" means a corporation in which the United States owns all the outstanding capital stock.

§ 30903. Waiver of immunity

(a) IN GENERAL—In a case in which, if a vessel were privately owned or operated, or if cargo were privately owned or possessed, or if a private person or property were involved, a civil action in admiralty could be maintained, a civil action in admiralty in personam may be brought against the United States or a federally-owned corporation. In a civil action in admiralty brought by the United States or a federally-owned corporation, an admiralty claim in personam may be filed or a setoff claimed against the United States or corporation.

(b) NON-JURY—A claim against the United States or a federally-owned corporation under this section shall be tried without a jury.

§ 30904. Exclusive remedy

If a remedy is provided by this chapter, it shall be exclusive of any other action arising out of the same subject matter against the officer, employee, or agent of the United States or the federally-owned corporation whose act or omission gave rise to the claim.

§ 30905. Period for bringing action

A civil action under this chapter must be brought within 2 years after the cause of action arose.

§ 30906. Venue

(a) IN GENERAL—A civil action under this chapter shall be brought in the district court of the United States for the district in which—

(1) any plaintiff resides or has its principal place of business; or

(2) the vessel or cargo is found.

(b) TRANSFER—On a motion by a party, the court may transfer the action to any other district court of the United States.

§ 30907. Procedure for hearing and determination

(a) IN GENERAL—A civil action under this chapter shall proceed and be heard and determined according to the principles of law and the rules of practice applicable in like cases between private parties.

(b) IN REM—

(1) REQUIREMENTS.—The action may proceed according to the principles of an action in rem if—

(A) the plaintiff elects in the complaint; and

(B) it appears that an action in rem could have been maintained had the vessel or cargo been privately owned and possessed.

(2) EFFECT ON RELIEF IN PERSONAM.—An election under paragraph (1) does not prevent the plaintiff from seeking relief in personam in the same action.

§ 30908. Exemption from arrest or seizure

The following are not subject to arrest or seizure by judicial process in the United States:

(1) A vessel owned by, possessed by, or operated by or for the United States or a federally-owned corporation.

(2) Cargo owned or possessed by the United States or a federally-owned corporation.

§ 30909. Security

Neither the United States nor a federally-owned corporation may be required to give a bond or admiralty stipulation in a civil action under this chapter.

§ 30910. Exoneration and limitation

The United States is entitled to the exemptions from and limitations of liability provided by law to an owner, charterer, operator, or agent of a vessel.

§ 30913. Payment of judgment or settlement

(a) IN GENERAL—The proper accounting officer of the United States shall pay a final judgment, arbitration award, or settlement under this chapter on presentation of an authenticated copy.

(b) SOURCE OF PAYMENT—Payment shall be made from an appropriation or fund available specifically for the purpose. If no appropriation or fund is specifically available, there is hereby appropriated, out of money in the Treasury not otherwise appropriated, an amount sufficient to pay the judgment, award, or settlement.

§ 30916. Recovery by the United States for salvage services

(a) CIVIL ACTION—The United States, and the crew of a merchant vessel owned or operated by the United States, or a federally-owned corporation, may bring a civil action to recover for salvage services provided by the vessel and crew.

(b) DEPOSIT OF AMOUNTS RECOVERED—Any amount recovered under this section by the United States for its own benefit, and not for the benefit of the crew, shall be deposited in the Treasury to the credit of the department of the United States Government, or the corporation, having control of the possession or operation of the vessel.

The Law Prior to the 2006 Recodification

Immediately prior to the 2006 recodification of Title 46, the Suits in Admiralty Act was included in the appendix to Title 46. See supra at 29.

Suits in Admiralty Act § 1, 46 U.S.C. app. § 741 (2000). [Exemption of United States vessels and cargoes from arrest or seizure]

No vessel owned by the United States or by any corporation in which the United States or its representatives shall own the entire outstanding capital stock or in the possession of the United States or of such corporation or operated by or for the United States or such corporation, and no cargo owned or possessed by the United States or by such corporation, shall hereafter, in view of the provision herein made for a libel in personam, be subject to arrest or seizure by judicial process in the United States or its possessions: *Provided*, That this Act shall not apply to the Panama Canal Commission.

Suits in Admiralty Act § 2, 46 U.S.C. app. § 742 (2000). [Libel in personam]

In cases where if such vessel were privately owned or operated, or if such cargo were privately owned or possessed, or if a private person or property were involved, a proceeding in admiralty could be maintained, any appropriate nonjury proceeding in personam may be brought against the United States or against any corporation mentioned in section 1 of this Act [former 46 U.S.C. app. § 741]. Such suits shall be brought in the district court of the United States for the district in which the parties so suing, or any of them, reside or have their principal place of business in the United States, or in which the vessel or cargo charged with liability is found. In case the United States or such corporation shall file a libel in rem or in personam in any district, a cross libel in personam may be filed or a set-off claimed against the United States or such corporation with the same force and effect as if the libel had been filed by a private party. Upon application of either party the cause may, in the discretion of the court, be transferred to any other district court of the United States.

Suits in Admiralty Act § 3, 46 U.S.C. app. § 743 (2000). [Procedure in cases of libel in personam]

Such suits shall proceed and shall be heard and determined according to the principles of law and to the rules of practice obtaining in like cases between private parties. A decree against the United States or such corporation[1] may include costs of suit, and when the decree is for a money judgment, interest at the rate of 4 per centum per annum until satisfied, or at any higher rate which shall be stipulated in any contract upon which such decree shall be based. Interest shall run as ordered by the court. Decrees shall be subject to appeal and revision as now provided in other cases of admiralty and maritime jurisdiction. If the libelant so elects in his libel, the suit may proceed in accordance with the principles of libels in rem wherever it shall appear that had the vessel or cargo been privately owned and possessed a libel in rem might have been maintained. Election so to proceed shall not preclude the libelant in any proper case from seeking relief in personam in the same suit. Neither the United States nor such corporation shall be required to give any bond or admiralty stipulation on any proceeding brought hereunder.

Suits in Admiralty Act § 5, 46 U.S.C. app. § 745 (2000). [Causes of action for which suits may be brought]

Suits as herein authorized may be brought only within two years after the cause of action arises: *Provided*, That where a remedy is provided by this Act it shall hereafter be exclusive of any other action by reason of the same subject matter against the agent or employee of the United States or of any incorporated or unincorporated agency thereof whose act or omission gave rise to the claim * * * .

---

1. Editors' note: The reference is presumably to "any corporation in which the United States or its representatives shall own the entire outstanding capital stock," as defined in section 1 of the Act, former 46 U.S.C. app. § 741. This was the view taken by the West Publishing Company when preparing *United States Code Annotated*, which substitutes the phrase "or a corporation mentioned in section 741 of this title" for the language that Congress enacted (which is reproduced in the United States Code). West Publishing Company made the same substitution in section 10, former 46 U.S.C. app. § 750, and a similar substitution in section 6, former 46 U.S.C. app. § 746.

Suits in Admiralty Act §6, 46 U.S.C. app. §746 (2000). [Exemptions and limitations of liability]

The United States or such corporation[2] shall be entitled to the benefits of all exemptions and of all limitations of liability accorded by law to the owners, charterers, operators, or agents of vessels.

Suits in Admiralty Act §10, 46 U.S.C. app. §750 (2000). [Recovery for salvage services by vessel or crew]

The United States, and the crew of any merchant vessel owned or operated by the United States, or such corporation,[3] shall have the right to collect and sue for salvage services rendered by such vessel and crew, and any moneys recovered therefrom by the United States for its own benefit, and not for the benefit of the crew, shall be covered into the United States Treasury[4] to the credit of the department of the Government of the United States, or of such corporation, having control of the possession or operation of such vessel.

---

2. Editors' note: *See supra* note 1.

3. Editors' note: *See supra* note 1.

4. Editors' note: "The phrase 'covered into the treasury,' as used in acts of Congress * * * , means that money has actually been paid into the treasury in the regular manner, as distinguished from merely depositing it with the treasurer." *Black's Law Dictionary* 365 (6th ed. 1990). The phrase is apparently unusual enough that it is not included in the current edition of *Black's Law Dictionary*.

Public Vessels Act

Congress originally enacted the Public Vessels Act, now codified at 46 U.S.C. §§ 31101–13, in 1925. 43 Stat. 1112. Section 10 was amended in 1954 to reduce the Attorney General's reporting responsibilities. The current language was enacted as chapter 311 of Title 46 as part of the 2006 recodification. See supra at 29.

§ 31101. Short title

This chapter may be cited as the "Public Vessels Act".

§ 31102. Waiver of immunity

(a) IN GENERAL—A civil action in personam in admiralty may be brought, or an impleader filed, against the United States for—

(1) damages caused by a public vessel of the United States; or

(2) compensation for towage and salvage services, including contract salvage, rendered to a public vessel of the United States.

(b) COUNTERCLAIM OR SETOFF—If the United States brings a civil action in admiralty for damages caused by a privately owned vessel, the owner of the vessel, or the successor in interest, may file a counterclaim in personam, or claim a setoff, against the United States for damages arising out of the same subject matter.

§ 31103. Applicable procedure

A civil action under this chapter is subject to the provisions of chapter 309 of this title except to the extent inconsistent with this chapter.

§ 31104. Venue

(a) IN GENERAL—A civil action under this chapter shall be brought in the district court of the United States for the district in which the vessel or cargo is found within the United States.

(b) VESSEL OR CARGO OUTSIDE TERRITORIAL WATERS—If the vessel or cargo is outside the territorial waters of the United States—

(1) the action shall be brought in the district court of the United States for any district in which any plaintiff resides or has an office for the transaction of business; or

(2) if no plaintiff resides or has an office for the transaction of business in the United States, the action may be brought in the district court of the United States for any district.

§ 31106. Exoneration and limitation

The United States is entitled to the exemptions from and limitations of liability provided by law to an owner, charterer, operator, or agent of a vessel.

§ 31107. Interest

A judgment in a civil action under this chapter may not include interest for the period before the judgment is issued unless the claim is based on a contract providing for interest.

§ 31110. Subpoenas to officers or members of crew

An officer or member of the crew of a public vessel may not be subpoenaed in a civil action under this chapter without the consent of—

(1) the Secretary of the department or the head of the independent establishment having control of the vessel at the time the cause of action arose; or

(2) the master or commanding officer of the vessel at the time the subpoena is issued.

§ 31111. Claims by nationals of foreign countries

A national of a foreign country may not maintain a civil action under this chapter unless it appears to the satisfaction of the court in which the action is brought that the government of that country, in similar circumstances, allows nationals of the United States to sue in its courts.

§ 31112. Lien not recognized or created

This chapter shall not be construed as recognizing the existence of or as creating a lien against a public vessel of the United States.

The Law Prior to the 2006 Recodification

Immediately prior to the 2006 recodification of Title 46, the Public Vessels Act was included in the appendix to Title 46. See supra at 29.

Public Vessels Act § 1, 46 U.S.C. app. § 781 (2000). [Libel in admiralty against or impleader of United States]

A libel in personam in admiralty may be brought against the United States, or a petition impleading the United States, for damages caused by a public vessel of the United States, and for compensation for towage and salvage services, including contract salvage, rendered to a public vessel of the United States: *Provided,* That the cause of action arose after the 6th day of April, 1920.

Public Vessels Act § 2, 46 U.S.C. app. § 782 (2000). [Venue of suit; application of Suits in Admiralty Act]

Such suit shall be brought in the district court of the United States for the district in which the vessel or cargo charged with creating the liability is found within the United States, or if such vessel or cargo be outside the territorial waters of the United States, then in the district court of the United States for the district in which the parties so suing, or any of them, reside or have an office for the transaction of business in the United States; or in case none of such parties reside or have an office for the transaction of business in the United States, and such vessel or cargo be outside the territorial waters of the United States, then in any district court of the United States. Such suits shall be subject to and proceed in accordance with the provisions of [the Suits in Admiralty Act, 46 U.S.C. §§ 30901–18 (previously codified at 46 U.S.C. app. §§ 741–752), *supra* at 53], or any amendment thereof, insofar as the same are not inconsistent herewith, except that no interest shall be allowed on any claim up to the time of the rendition of judgment unless upon a contract expressly stipulating for the payment of interest.

Public Vessels Act § 4, 46 U.S.C. app. § 784 (2000). [Subpoenas to officers or members of crew]

No officer or member of the crew of any public vessel of the United States may be subpoenaed in connection with any suit authorized under this Act without the consent of the Secretary of the department or the head of any independent establishment of the Government having control of the vessel at the time the cause of action arose, or of the master or commanding officer of such vessel at the time of the issuance of such subpoena.

Public Vessels Act § 5, 46 U.S.C. app. § 785 (2000). [Suits by nationals of foreign governments]

No suit may be brought under this Act by a national of any foreign government unless it shall appear to the satisfaction of the court in which suit is brought that said government, under similar circumstances, allows nationals of the United States to sue in its courts.

Public Vessels Act § 8, 46 U.S.C. app. § 788 (2000). [Lien not created against public vessels]

Nothing contained in this Act shall be construed to recognize the existence of or as creating a lien against any public vessel of the United States.

Public Vessels Act § 9, 46 U.S.C. app. § 789 (2000). [Exemptions and limitations of liability]

The United States shall be entitled to the benefits of all exemptions and of all limitations of liability accorded by law to the owners, charterers, operators or agents of vessels.

Federal Maritime Lien Act;
Ship Mortgage Act

In 1910, Congress passed the Federal Maritime Lien Act (FMLA), 36 Stat. 604. FMLA was then incorporated into the Ship Mortgage Act, 1920, 41 Stat. 1000. The combined statutes were then recodified as part of the ongoing revision of Title 46 of the United States Code, 46 U.S.C. §§ 31301–43, and this recodification was enacted into positive law in 1988. 102 Stat. 4735. Selected provisions are reproduced here.

46 U.S.C. § 31301. Definitions

In this chapter[1]—

* * *

(3) "mortgagee" means—

(A) a person to whom property is mortgaged; or

(B) when a mortgage on a vessel involves a trust, the trustee that is designated in the trust agreement;

(4) "necessaries" includes repairs, supplies, towage, and the use of a dry dock or marine railway;

(5) "preferred maritime lien" means a maritime lien on a vessel—

(A) arising before a preferred mortgage was filed under [46 U.S.C. § 31321];

(B) for damage arising out of maritime tort;

(C) for wages of a stevedore when employed directly by a person listed in [46 U.S.C. § 31341];

(D) for wages of the crew of the vessel;

(E) for general average; or

(F) for salvage, including contract salvage[.]

* * *

46 U.S.C. § 31305. Waiver of lien rights

This chapter[2] does not prevent a mortgagee or other lien holder from waiving or subordinating at any time by agreement or otherwise the lien holder's right to a lien, the priority or, if a preferred mortgage lien, the preferred status of the lien.

46 U.S.C. § 31307. State statutes superseded

This chapter[3] supersedes any State statute conferring a lien on a vessel to the extent the statute establishes a claim to be enforced by a civil action in rem against the vessel for necessaries.

---

1. Editors' note: The reference is to chapter 313 of Title 46, titled "Commercial Instruments and Maritime Liens," 46 U.S.C. §§ 31301–43.

2. Editors' note: The reference is to chapter 313 of Title 46, titled "Commercial Instruments and Maritime Liens," 46 U.S.C. §§ 31301–43.

3. Editors' note: The reference is to chapter 313 of Title 46, titled "Commercial Instruments and Maritime Liens," 46 U.S.C. §§ 31301–43.

46 U.S.C. § 31322. Preferred mortgages

(a) A preferred mortgage is a mortgage, whenever made, that—

(1) includes the whole of the vessel;

(2) is filed in substantial compliance with [46 U.S.C. § 31321]; and

(3) (A) covers a documented vessel; or

(B) covers a vessel for which an application for documentation is filed that is in substantial compliance with the requirements of chapter 121[4] of this title and the regulations prescribed under that chapter.

* * *

46 U.S.C. § 31326. Court sales to enforce preferred mortgage liens and maritime liens and priority of claims

(a) When a vessel is sold by order of a district court in a civil action in rem brought to enforce a preferred mortgage lien or a maritime lien, any claim in the vessel existing on the date of sale is terminated, including a possessory common law lien of which a person is deprived under [46 U.S.C. § 31325(e)(2)], and the vessel is sold free of all those claims.

(b) Each of the claims terminated under subsection (a) of this section attaches, in the same amount and in accordance with their priorities to the proceeds of the sale, except that—

(1) the preferred mortgage lien, including a preferred mortgage lien on a foreign vessel whose mortgage has been guaranteed under title XI of the Merchant Marine Act, 1936 [46 U.S.C. §§ 53701 *et seq.* (previously codified at 46 U.S.C. app. §§ 1271–1279e)], has priority over all claims against the vessel (except for expenses and fees allowed by the court, costs imposed by the court, and preferred maritime liens); and

(2) for a foreign vessel whose mortgage has not been guaranteed under title XI of that Act, the preferred mortgage lien is subordinate to a maritime lien for necessaries provided in the United States.

46 U.S.C. § 31341. Persons presumed to have authority to procure necessaries

(a) The following persons are presumed to have authority to procure necessaries for a vessel:

(1) the owner;

(2) the master;

(3) a person entrusted with the management of the vessel at the port of supply; or

(4) an officer or agent appointed by—

(A) the owner;

(B) a charterer;

(C) an owner pro hac vice; or

---

4. Editors' note: The reference is to chapter 121 of Title 46, titled "Documentation of Vessels," 46 U.S.C. §§ 12101–24.

(D) an agreed buyer in possession of the vessel.

(b) A person tortiously or unlawfully in possession or charge of a vessel has no authority to procure necessaries for the vessel.

46 U.S.C. § 31342. Establishing maritime liens

(a) Except as provided in subsection (b) of this section, a person providing necessaries to a vessel on the order of the owner or a person authorized by the owner—

(1) has a maritime lien on the vessel;

(2) may bring a civil action in rem to enforce the lien; and

(3) is not required to allege or prove in the action that credit was given to the vessel.

(b) This section does not apply to a public vessel.

46 U.S.C. § 31343. Recording and discharging liens on preferred mortgage vessels

(a) Except as provided under subsection (d) of this section, a person claiming a lien on a vessel documented, or for which an application for documentation has been filed, under chapter 121[5] may record with the Secretary of Transportation a notice of that person's lien claim on the vessel. To be recordable, the notice must—

(1) state the nature of the lien;

(2) state the date the lien was established;

(3) state the amount of the lien;

(4) state the name and address of the person; and

(5) be signed and acknowledged.

(b) (1) The Secretary shall record a notice complying with subsection (a) of this section if, when the notice is presented to the Secretary for recording, the person having the claim files with the notice a declaration stating the following:

(A) The information in the notice is true and correct to the best of the knowledge, information, and belief of the individual who signed it.

(B) A copy of the notice, as presented for recordation, has been sent to each of the following:

(i) The owner of the vessel.

(ii) Each person that recorded under subsection (a) of this section an unexpired notice of a claim of an undischarged lien on the vessel.

(iii) The mortgagee of each mortgage filed or recorded under section 31321 of this title that is an undischarged mortgage on the vessel.

(2) A declaration under this subsection filed by a person that is not an individual must be signed by the president, member, partner, trustee, or other individual authorized to execute the declaration on behalf of the person.

(c) (1) On full and final discharge of the indebtedness that is the basis for a notice of claim of lien recorded under subsection (b) of this section, the person having the claim

---

5. Editors' note: The reference is to chapter 121 of Title 46, titled "Documentation of Vessels," 46 U.S.C. §§ 12101–24.

shall provide the Secretary with an acknowledged certificate of discharge of the indebtedness. The Secretary shall record the certificate.

(2) The district courts of the United States shall have jurisdiction over a civil action in Admiralty to declare that a vessel is not subject to a lien claimed under subsection (b) of this section, or that the vessel is not subject to the notice of claim of lien, or both, regardless of the amount in controversy or the citizenship of the parties. Venue in such an action shall be in the district where the vessel is found or where the claimant resides or where the notice of claim of lien is recorded. The court may award costs and attorneys fees to the prevailing party, unless the court finds that the position of the other party was substantially justified or other circumstances make an award of costs and attorneys fees unjust. The Secretary shall record any such declaratory order.

(d) A person claiming a lien on a vessel covered by a preferred mortgage under [46 U.S.C. §31322(d)] must record and discharge the lien as provided by the law of the State in which the vessel is titled.

(e) A notice of claim of lien recorded under subsection (b) of this section shall expire 3 years after the date the lien was established, as such date is stated in the notice under subsection (a) of this section.

(f) This section does not alter in any respect the law pertaining to the establishment of a maritime lien, the remedy provided by such a lien, or the defenses thereto, including any defense under the doctrine of laches.

Salvage Act

Congress originally enacted the Salvage Act, now codified at 46 U.S.C. § 80107, in 1912, 37 Stat. 242, in conjunction with the ratification of the 1910 Brussels Convention for the Unification of Certain Rules of Law Relating to Assistance and Salvage at Sea, 37 Stat. 1658. Section 2 of the original Salvage Act, previously codified at 46 U.S.C. § 728, was repealed in 1983, when it was superseded by 46 U.S.C. § 2304 (supra at 30). The current language of the Salvage Act was enacted as part of the 2006 recodification of Title 46. See supra at 29.

§ 80107. Salvors of life to share in remuneration

(a) ENTITLEMENT OF SALVORS—A salvor of human life, who gave aid following an accident giving rise to salvage, is entitled to a fair share of the payment awarded to the salvor for salvaging the vessel or other property or preventing or minimizing damage to the environment.

(b) COMMON OWNERSHIP OF VESSELS—The right to remuneration for aid or salvage services is not affected by common ownership of the vessels giving and receiving the aid or salvage services.

(c) TIME LIMIT ON BRINGING ACTIONS—A civil action to recover remuneration for giving aid or salvage services must be brought within 2 years after the date the aid or salvage services were given, unless the court in which the action is brought is satisfied that during that 2-year period there had not been a reasonable opportunity to seize the aided or salvaged vessel within the jurisdiction of the court or within the territorial waters of the country of the plaintiff's residence or principal place of business.

(d) NONAPPLICATION—This section does not apply to a vessel of war or a vessel owned by the United States Government appropriated only to a public service.

The Law Prior to the 2006 Recodification

Immediately prior to the 2006 recodification of Title 46, the Salvage Act was included in the appendix to Title 46. See supra at 29.

Salvage Act § 1, 46 U.S.C. app. § 727 (2000). Right to salvage not affected by ownership of vessel

The right to remuneration for assistance or salvage services shall not be affected by common ownership of the vessels rendering and receiving such assistance or salvage services.

Salvage Act § 3, 46 U.S.C. app. § 729 (2000). Salvors of life to share in remuneration

Salvors of human life, who have taken part in the services rendered on the occasion of the accident giving rise to salvage, are entitled to a fair share of the payment awarded to the salvor for salving the vessel or other property or preventing or minimizing damage to the environment.

Salvage Act § 4, 46 U.S.C. app. § 730 (2000). Time limit for salvage suits

A suit for the recovery of remuneration for rendering assistance or salvage services shall not be maintainable if brought later than two years from the date when such assistance or salvage was rendered, unless the court in which the suit is brought shall be satisfied that during such period there had not been any reasonable opportunity of arresting the assisted or salved vessel within the jurisdiction of the court or within the territorial waters of the country in which the libelant resides or has his principal place of business.

Salvage Act § 5, 46 U.S.C. app. § 731 (2000). Applicability to ships of war

Nothing in sections 1, 3, and 4 of this Act [former 46 U.S.C. app. §§ 727, 729, 730] and [46 U.S.C. § 2304] shall be construed as applying to ships of war or to Government ships appropriated exclusively to a public service.

Carriage of Goods by Sea Act

Congress enacted the Carriage of Goods by Sea Act ("COGSA"), in 1936. 49 Stat. 1207. Although significant amendments have been discussed for many years, Congress has not amended the Act in any substantive way since it was first passed.

When Congress completed the recodification of Title 46 in 2006, COGSA was not included in the recodification. Because the United States was then participating in international negotiations to modernize the Hague Rules, the international convention on which COGSA is based, it was considered inappropriate for Congress unilaterally to modernize the domestic statute. See Michael F. Sturley, Reflections on the Recodification of Title 46, 2 BENEDICT's MARITIME BULLETIN 209 (2004). As a result, COGSA simply dropped out of title 46 and became an un-codified statute (pending the completion of the international negotiations). It remains in force, but appears in the U.S. Code only as a note within the recodified Harter Act (see supra at 49).

COGSA Enacting Clause, previously codified at 46 U.S.C. app. § 1300 (2000). [Bills of lading subject to COGSA]

Every bill of lading or similar document of title which is evidence of a contract for the carriage of goods by sea to or from ports of the United States, in foreign trade, shall have effect subject to the provisions of this Act.

COGSA § 1, previously codified at 46 U.S.C. app. § 1301 (2000). [Definitions]

When used in this Act—

(a) The term "carrier" includes the owner or the charterer who enters into a contract of carriage with a shipper.

(b) The term "contract of carriage" applies only to contracts of carriage covered by a bill of lading or any similar document of title, insofar as such document relates to the carriage of goods by sea, including any bill of lading or any similar document as aforesaid issued under or pursuant to a charter party from the moment at which such bill of lading or similar document of title regulates the relations between a carrier and a holder of the same.

(c) The term "goods" includes goods, wares, merchandise, and articles of every kind whatsoever, except live animals and cargo which by the contract of carriage is stated as being carried on deck and is so carried.

(d) The term "ship" means any vessel used for the carriage of goods by sea.

(e) The term "carriage of goods" covers the period from the time when the goods are loaded on to the time when they are discharged from the ship.

COGSA § 2, previously codified at 46 U.S.C. app. § 1302 (2000). Risks [Duties and rights of carrier]

Subject to the provisions of section 6 [previously codified at 46 U.S.C. app. § 1306], under every contract of carriage of goods by sea, the carrier in relation to the loading, handling, stowage, carriage, custody, care, and discharge of such goods, shall be subject to the responsibilities and liabilities and entitled to the rights and immunities hereinafter set forth.

COGSA § 3, previously codified at 46 U.S.C. app. § 1303 (2000). Responsibilities and liabilities [of carrier and ship]

(1) The carrier shall be bound, before and at the beginning of the voyage, to exercise due diligence to—

(a) Make the ship seaworthy;

(b) Properly man, equip, and supply the ship;

(c) Make the holds, refrigerating and cooling chambers, and all other parts of the ship in which goods are carried, fit and safe for their reception, carriage, and preservation.

(2) The carrier shall properly and carefully load, handle, stow, carry, keep, care for, and discharge the goods carried.

(3) After receiving the goods into his charge the carrier, or the master or agent of the carrier, shall, on demand of the shipper, issue to the shipper a bill of lading showing among other things—

(a) The leading marks necessary for identification of the goods as the same are furnished in writing by the shipper before the loading of such goods starts, provided such marks are stamped or otherwise shown clearly upon the goods if uncovered, or on the cases or coverings in which such goods are contained, in such a manner as should ordinarily remain legible until the end of the voyage.

(b) Either the number of packages or pieces, or the quantity or weight, as the case may be, as furnished in writing by the shipper.

(c) The apparent order and condition of the goods;

Provided, That no carrier, master, or agent of the carrier, shall be bound to state or show in the bill of lading any marks, number, quantity, or weight which he has reasonable ground for suspecting not accurately to represent the goods actually received, or which he has had no reasonable means of checking.

(4) Such a bill of lading shall be prima facie evidence of the receipt by the carrier of the goods as therein described in accordance with paragraphs (3)(a), (b), and (c), of this section: *Provided*, That nothing in this Act shall be construed as repealing or limiting the application of any part of the [Federal Bill of Lading Act, popularly known as the Pomerene Act, 49 U.S.C. §§ 80101–16].

(5) The shipper shall be deemed to have guaranteed to the carrier the accuracy at the time of shipment of the marks, number, quantity, and weight, as furnished by him; and the shipper shall indemnify the carrier against all loss, damages, and expenses arising or resulting from inaccuracies in such particulars. The right of the carrier to such indemnity shall in no way limit his responsibility and liability under the contract of carriage to any person other than the shipper.

(6) Unless notice of loss or damage and the general nature of such loss or damage be given in writing to the carrier or his agent at the port of discharge before or at the time of the removal of the goods into the custody of the person entitled to delivery thereof under the contract of carriage, such removal shall be prima facie evidence of the delivery by the carrier of the goods as described in the bill of lading. If the loss or damage is not apparent, the notice must be given within three days of the delivery.

Said notice of loss or damage may be endorsed upon the receipt for the goods given by the person taking delivery thereof.

The notice in writing need not be given if the state of the goods has at the time of their receipt been the subject of joint survey or inspection.

In any event the carrier and the ship shall be discharged from all liability in respect of loss or damage unless suit is brought within one year after delivery of the goods or the date when the goods should have been delivered: *Provided*, That if a notice of loss or damage, either apparent or concealed, is not given as provided for in this section, that fact shall not affect or prejudice the right of the shipper to bring suit within one year after the delivery of the goods or the date when the goods should have been delivered.

In the case of any actual or apprehended loss or damage the carrier and the receiver shall give all reasonable facilities to each other for inspecting and tallying the goods.

(7) After the goods are loaded the bill of lading to be issued by the carrier, master, or agent of the carrier to the shipper shall, if the shipper so demands, be a "shipped" bill of lading: *Provided*, That if the shipper shall have previously taken up any document of title to such goods, he shall surrender the same as against the issue of the "shipped" bill of lading, but at the option of the carrier such document of title may be noted at the port of shipment by the carrier, master, or agent with the name or names of the ship or ships upon which the goods have been shipped and the date or dates of shipment, and when so noted the same shall for the purpose of this section be deemed to constitute a "shipped" bill of lading.

(8) Any clause, covenant, or agreement in a contract of carriage relieving the carrier or the ship from liability for loss or damage to or in connection with the goods, arising from negligence, fault, or failure in the duties and obligations provided in this section, or lessening such liability otherwise than as provided in this Act, shall be null and void and of no effect. A benefit of insurance in favor of the carrier, or similar clause, shall be deemed to be a clause relieving the carrier from liability.

COGSA § 4, previously codified at 46 U.S.C. app. § 1304 (2000). Rights and immunities [of carrier and ship]

(1) Neither the carrier nor the ship shall be liable for loss or damage arising or resulting from unseaworthiness unless caused by want of due diligence on the part of the carrier to make the ship seaworthy, and to secure that the ship is properly manned, equipped, and supplied, and to make the holds, refrigerating and cool chambers, and all other parts of the ship in which goods are carried fit and safe for their reception, carriage, and preservation in accordance with the provisions of paragraph (1) of section 3. Whenever loss or damage has resulted from unseaworthiness, the burden of proving the exercise of due diligence shall be on the carrier or other persons claiming exemption under this section.

(2) Neither the carrier nor the ship shall be responsible for loss or damage arising or resulting from—

(a) Act, neglect, or default of the master, mariner, pilot, or the servants of the carrier in the navigation or in the management of the ship;

(b) Fire, unless caused by the actual fault or privity of the carrier;

(c) Perils, dangers, and accidents of the sea or other navigable waters;

(d) Act of God;

(e) Act of war;

(f) Act of public enemies;

(g) Arrest or restraint of princes, rulers, or people, or seizure under legal process;

(h) Quarantine restrictions;

(i) Act or omission of the shipper or owner of the goods, his agent or representative;

(j) Strikes or lockouts or stoppage or restraint of labor from whatever cause, whether partial or general: *Provided*, that nothing herein contained shall be construed to relieve a carrier from responsibility for the carrier's own acts;

(k) Riots and civil commotions;

(l) Saving or attempting to save life or property at sea;

(m) Wastage in bulk or weight or any other loss or damage arising from inherent defect, quality, or vice of the goods;

(n) Insufficiency of packing;

(o) Insufficiency or inadequacy of marks;

(p) Latent defects not discoverable by due diligence; and

(q) Any other cause arising without the actual fault and privity of the carrier and without the fault or neglect of the agents or servants of the carrier, but the burden of proof shall be on the person claiming the benefit of this exception to show that neither the actual fault or privity of the carrier nor the fault or neglect of the agents or servants of the carrier contributed to the loss or damage.

(3) The shipper shall not be responsible for loss or damage sustained by the carrier or the ship arising or resulting from any cause without the act, fault, or neglect of the shipper, his agents, or his servants.

(4) Any deviation in saving or attempting to save life or property at sea, or any reasonable deviation shall not be deemed to be an infringement or breach of this Act or of the contract of carriage, and the carrier shall not be liable for any loss or damage resulting therefrom: *Provided, however,* That if the deviation is for the purpose of loading or unloading cargo or passengers it shall, prima facie, be regarded as unreasonable.

(5) Neither the carrier nor the ship shall in any event be or become liable for any loss or damage to or in connection with the transportation of goods in an amount exceeding $500 per package lawful money of the United States, or in case of goods not shipped in packages, per customary freight unit, or the equivalent of that sum in other currency, unless the nature and value of such goods have been declared by the shipper before shipment and inserted in the bill of lading. This declaration, if embodied in the bill of lading, shall be prima facie evidence, but shall not be conclusive on the carrier.

By agreement between the carrier, master, or agent of the carrier, and the shipper another maximum amount than that mentioned in this paragraph may be fixed: *Provided,* That such maximum shall not be less than the figure above named. In no event shall the carrier be liable for more than the amount of damage actually sustained.

Neither the carrier nor the ship shall be responsible in any event for loss or damage to or in connection with the transportation of the goods if the nature or value thereof has been knowingly and fraudulently misstated by the shipper in the bill of lading.

(6) Goods of an inflammable, explosive, or dangerous nature to the shipment whereof the carrier, master or agent of the carrier, has not consented with knowledge of their nature and character, may at any time before discharge be landed at any place or destroyed or rendered innocuous by the carrier without compensation, and the shipper of such goods shall be liable for all damages and expenses directly or indirectly arising out of or resulting from such shipment. If any such goods shipped with such knowledge and consent shall become a danger to the ship or cargo, they may in like manner be landed at any place, or destroyed or rendered innocuous by the carrier without liability on the part of the carrier except to general average, if any.

COGSA § 5, previously codified at 46 U.S.C. app. § 1305 (2000). Surrender of rights and immunities and increase of responsibility and liabilities [charter parties; general average]

A carrier shall be at liberty to surrender in whole or in part all or any of his rights and immunities or to increase any of his responsibilities and liabilities under this Act, provided such surrender or increase shall be embodied in the bill of lading issued to the shipper.

The provisions of this Act shall not be applicable to charter parties; but if bills of lading are issued in the case of a ship under a charter party, they shall comply with the terms of this Act. Nothing in this Act shall be held to prevent the insertion in a bill of lading of any lawful provision regarding general average.

COGSA § 6, previously codified at 46 U.S.C. app. § 1306 (2000). Special conditions

Notwithstanding the provisions of the preceding sections, a carrier, master or agent of the carrier, and a shipper shall, in regard to any particular goods be at liberty to enter into any agreement in any terms as to the responsibility and liability of the carrier for such goods, and as to the rights and immunities of the carrier in respect of such goods, or his obligation as to seaworthiness (so far as the stipulation regarding seaworthiness is not contrary to public policy), or the care or diligence of his servants or agents in regard to the loading, handling, stowage, carriage, custody, care, and discharge of the goods carried by sea: *Provided*, That in this case no bill of lading has been or shall be issued and that the terms agreed shall be embodied in a receipt which shall be a nonnegotiable document and shall be marked as such.

Any agreement so entered into shall have full legal effect: *Provided*, That this section shall not apply to ordinary commercial shipments made in the ordinary course of trade but only to other shipments where the character or condition of the property to be carried or the circumstances, terms, and conditions under which the carriage is to be performed are such as reasonably to justify a special agreement.

COGSA § 7, previously codified at 46 U.S.C. app. § 1307 (2000). [Agreement as to liability prior to loading or after discharge]

Nothing contained in this Act shall prevent a carrier or a shipper from entering into any agreement, stipulation, condition, reservation, or exemption as to the responsibility and liability of the carrier or the ship for the loss or damage to or in connection with the custody and care and handling of goods prior to the loading on and subsequent to the discharge from the ship on which the goods are carried by sea.

COGSA § 8, previously codified at 46 U.S.C. app. § 1308 (2000). [Rights and liabilities under other provisions]

The provisions of this Act shall not affect the rights and obligations of the carrier under the provisions of the Shipping Act, 1916, or under the provisions of [the Limitation Act, 46 U.S.C. §§ 30501–12 (previously codified at 46 U.S.C. app. §§ 181–188), *supra* at 41], or of any amendments thereto; or under the provisions of any other enactment for the time being in force relating to the limitation of the liability of the owners of seagoing vessels.

COGSA § 9, previously codified at 46 U.S.C. app. § 1309 (2000). [Discrimination between competing shippers]

Nothing contained in this Act shall be construed as permitting a common carrier by water to discriminate between competing shippers similarly placed in time and circumstances, either (a) with respect to their right to demand and receive bills of lading subject to the provisions of this Act; or (b) when issuing such bills of lading, either in the surrender of any of the carrier's rights and immunities or in the increase of any of the carrier's responsibilities and liabilities pursuant to section 5 * * * of this Act [previously codified at 46 U.S.C. app. § 1305]; or (c) in any other way prohibited by the Shipping Act, 1916, as amended.

COGSA § 11, previously codified at 46 U.S.C. app. § 1310 (2000). [Weight of bulk cargo]

Where under the customs of any trade the weight of any bulk cargo inserted in the bill of lading is a weight ascertained or accepted by a third party other than the carrier or the shipper, and the fact that the weight is so ascertained or accepted is stated in the bill of lading, then, notwithstanding anything in this Act, the bill of lading shall not be deemed to be prima facie evidence against the carrier of the receipt of goods of the weight so inserted in the bill of lading, and the accuracy thereof at the time of shipment shall not be deemed to have been guaranteed by the shipper.

COGSA § 12, previously codified at 46 U.S.C. app. § 1311 (2000). [Liabilities before loading or after discharge; effect on other laws]

Nothing in this Act shall be construed as superseding any part of the [Harter Act, 46 U.S.C. §§ 30701–07 (previously codified at 46 U.S.C. app. §§ 190–196), *supra* at 49], or of any other law which would be applicable in the absence of this Act, insofar as they relate to the duties, responsibilities, and liabilities of the ship or carrier prior to the time when the goods are loaded on or after the time they are discharged from the ship.

COGSA § 13, previously codified at 46 U.S.C. app. § 1312 (2000). [Scope of chapter; "United States"; "foreign trade"]

This Act shall apply to all contracts for carriage of goods by sea to or from ports of the United States in foreign trade. As used in this Act the term "United States" includes its districts, territories, and possessions. The term "foreign trade" means the transportation of goods between the ports of the United States and ports of foreign countries. Nothing in this Act shall be held to apply to contracts for carriage of goods by sea between any port of the United States or its possessions, and any other port of the United States or its possessions: *Provided, however,* That any bill of lading or similar document of title which is evidence of a contract for the carriage of goods by sea between such ports, containing an express statement that it shall be subject to the provisions of this Act, shall be subjected hereto as fully as if subject hereto by the express provisions of this Act; *Provided further,* That every bill of lading or similar document of title which is evidence of a contract for the carriage of goods by sea from ports of the United States, in foreign trade, shall contain a statement that it shall have effect subject to the provisions of this Act.

Federal Rules of Civil Procedure

The Federal Rules of Civil Procedure, promulgated in 1938, originally applied to actions at law and in equity. The Rules were extended to admiralty actions in 1966. Supplemental Rules A–F, which were specifically included in the rules for admiralty cases, preserved some of the unique aspects of the pre-existing admiralty practice. A few other rules are particularly relevant in admiralty cases. The principal relevant provisions are reproduced here.

Minor revisions to the Rules to introduce "plain-English style conventions" took effect on December 1, 2007. Those revisions were intended to simplify and clarify the Rules without changing their current substance. Thus it may be helpful to have both the current and former language of the Rules available. In any event, most of the cases included in the casebook were decided before the current Rules took effect, and the courts would therefore have been applying the previous language.

FED. R. CIV. P. 4(k). TERRITORIAL LIMITS OF EFFECTIVE SERVICE.

(1) **In General.** Serving a summons or filing a waiver of service establishes personal jurisdiction over a defendant:

(A) who is subject to the jurisdiction of a court of general jurisdiction in the state where the district court is located;

(B) who is a party joined under Rule 14 or 19 and is served within a judicial district of the United States and not more than 100 miles from where the summons was issued; or

(C) when authorized by a federal statute.

(2) **Federal Claim Outside State-Court Jurisdiction.** For a claim that arises under federal law, serving a summons or filing a waiver of service establishes personal jurisdiction over a defendant if:

(A) the defendant is not subject to jurisdiction in any state's courts of general jurisdiction; and

(B) exercising jurisdiction is consistent with the United States Constitution and laws.

FED. R. CIV. P. 9(h). ADMIRALTY AND MARITIME CLAIMS.

(1) **How Designated.** If a claim for relief is within the admiralty or maritime jurisdiction and also within the court's subject-matter jurisdiction on some other ground, the pleading may designate the claim as an admiralty or maritime claim for purposes of Rules 14(c), 38(e), and 82 and the Supplemental Rules for Admiralty or Maritime Claims and Asset Forfeiture Actions. A claim cognizable only in the admiralty or maritime jurisdiction is an admiralty or maritime claim for those purposes, whether or not so designated.

(2) **Designation for Appeal.** A case that includes an admiralty or maritime claim within this subdivision (h) is an admiralty case within 28 U.S.C. § 1292(a)(3).

FED. R. CIV. P. 14. THIRD-PARTY PRACTICE.

(a) WHEN A DEFENDING PARTY MAY BRING IN A THIRD PARTY.

(1) **Timing of the Summons and Complaint.** A defending party may, as third-party plaintiff, serve a summons and complaint on a nonparty who is or may be liable to it for all or part of the claim against it. * * *

* * *

(c) ADMIRALTY OR MARITIME CLAIM.

(1) **Scope of Impleader.** If a plaintiff asserts an admiralty or maritime claim under Rule 9(h), the defendant or a person who asserts a right under Supplemental Rule C(6)(a)(i) may, as a third-party plaintiff, bring in a third-party defendant who may be wholly or partly liable—either to the plaintiff or to the third-party plaintiff—for remedy over, contribution, or otherwise on account of the same transaction, occurrence, or series of transactions or occurrences.

(2) **Defending Against a Demand for Judgment for the Plaintiff.** The third-party plaintiff may demand judgment in the plaintiff's favor against the third-party defendant. In that event, the third-party defendant must defend under Rule 12 against the plaintiff's claim as well as the third-party plaintiff's claim; and the action proceeds as if the plaintiff had sued both the third-party defendant and the third-party plaintiff.

FED. R. CIV. P. 38. RIGHT TO A JURY TRIAL; DEMAND.

(a) RIGHT PRESERVED. The right of trial by jury as declared by the Seventh Amendment to the Constitution—or as provided by a federal statute—is preserved to the parties inviolate.

* * *

(e) ADMIRALTY AND MARITIME CLAIMS. These rules do not create a right to a jury trial on issues in a claim that is an admiralty or maritime claim under Rule 9(h).

FED. R. CIV. P. 82. JURISDICTION AND VENUE UNAFFECTED.

These rules do not extend or limit the jurisdiction of the district courts or the venue of actions in those courts. An admiralty or maritime claim under Rule 9(h) is not a civil action for purposes of 28 U.S.C. §§ 1391–1392.

SUPPLEMENTAL RULES FOR CERTAIN ADMIRALTY AND MARITIME CLAIMS

RULE A. SCOPE OF RULES.

(1) These Supplemental Rules apply to:

(A) the procedure in admiralty and maritime claims within the meaning of Rule 9(h) with respect to the following remedies:

(i) maritime attachment and garnishment,

(ii) actions in rem,

(iii) possessory, petitory, and partition actions, and

(iv) actions for exoneration from or limitation of liability;

* * *

(2) The Federal Rules of Civil Procedure also apply to the foregoing proceedings except to the extent that they are inconsistent with these Supplemental Rules.

Rule B. Attachment and Garnishment: Special Provisions.

(1) When Available; Complaint, Affidavit, Judicial Authorization, and Process. In an in personam action:

(a) If a defendant is <u>not found within the district when a verified complaint praying for attachment and the affidavit required by Rule B(1)(b) are fi</u>led, a verified complaint may contain a prayer for process to attach the defendant's tangible or intangible personal property—up to the amount sued for—in the hands of garnishees named in the process.

(b) The plaintiff or the plaintiff's attorney must sign and file with the complaint an affidavit stating that, to the affiant's knowledge, or on information and belief, the defendant cannot be found within the district. The court must review the complaint and affidavit and, if the conditions of this Rule B appear to exist, enter an order so stating and authorizing process of attachment and garnishment. The clerk may issue supplemental process enforcing the court's order upon application without further court order.

(c) If the plaintiff or the plaintiff's attorney certifies that <u>exigent circumstances</u> *= Alaska* make court review impracticable, the clerk must issue the <u>summons and process of</u> attachment and garnishment. The plaintiff has the burden in any post-attachment hearing under Rule E(4)(f) to show that exigent circumstances existed.

(d) (i) If the property is a vessel or tangible property on board a vessel, the summons, process, and any supplemental process must be delivered to the marshal for service.

(ii) If the property is other tangible or intangible property, the summons, process, and any supplemental process must be delivered to a person or organization authorized to serve it, who may be (A) a marshal; (B) someone under contract with the United States; (C) someone specially appointed by the court for that purpose; or, (D) in an action brought by the United States, any officer or employee of the United States.

(e) The plaintiff may invoke state-law remedies under Rule 64 for seizure of person or property for the purpose of securing satisfaction of the judgment.

(2) Notice to Defendant. No default judgment may be entered except upon proof—which may be by affidavit—that:

(a) the complaint, summons, and process of attachment or garnishment have been served on the defendant in a manner authorized by Rule 4;

(b) the plaintiff or the garnishee has mailed to the defendant the complaint, summons, and process of attachment or garnishment, using any form of mail requiring a return receipt; or

(c) the plaintiff or the garnishee has tried diligently to give notice of the action to the defendant but could not do so.

(3) Answer.

(a) By Garnishee. The garnishee shall serve an answer, together with answers to any interrogatories served with the complaint, within 20 days after service of process upon the garnishee. Interrogatories to the garnishee may be served with the complaint without leave of court. If the garnishee refuses or neglects to answer on oath as to the debts, credits, or effects of the defendant in the garnishee's hands, or any interrogatories concerning such debts, credits, and effects that may be propounded by the plaintiff, the court may award compulsory process against the garnishee. If the garnishee admits any debts, credits, or effects, they shall be held in the garnishee's hands or paid into the registry of the court, and shall be held in either case subject to the further order of the court.

(b) By DEFENDANT. The defendant shall serve an answer within 30 days after process has been executed, whether by attachment of property or service on the garnishee.

RULE C. ACTIONS IN REM: SPECIAL PROVISIONS.

(1) WHEN AVAILABLE. An action in rem may be brought:

(a) To enforce any maritime lien;

(b) Whenever a statute of the United States provides for a maritime action in rem or a proceeding analogous thereto.

Except as otherwise provided by law a party who may proceed in rem may also, or in the alternative, proceed in personam against any person who may be liable.

Statutory provisions exempting vessels or other property owned or possessed by or operated by or for the United States from arrest or seizure are not affected by this rule. When a statute so provides, an action against the United States or an instrumentality thereof may proceed on in rem principles.

(2) COMPLAINT. In an action in rem the complaint must:

(a) be verified;

(b) describe with reasonable particularity the property that is the subject of the action; and

(c) in an admiralty and maritime proceeding, state that the property is within the district or will be within the district while the action is pending.

(3) JUDICIAL AUTHORIZATION AND PROCESS.

(a) ARREST WARRANT.

(i) The court must review the complaint and any supporting papers. If the conditions for an in rem action appear to exist, the court must issue an order directing the clerk to issue a warrant for the arrest of the vessel or other property that is the subject of the action.

(ii) If the plaintiff or the plaintiff's attorney certifies that exigent circumstances make court review impracticable, the clerk must promptly issue a summons and a warrant for the arrest of the vessel or other property that is the subject of the action. The plaintiff has the burden in any post-arrest hearing under Rule E(4)(f) to show that exigent circumstances existed.

(b) SERVICE.

(i) If the property that is the subject of the action is a vessel or tangible property on board a vessel, the warrant and any supplemental process must be delivered to the marshal for service.

(ii) If the property that is the subject of the action is other property, tangible or intangible, the warrant and any supplemental process must be delivered to a person or organization authorized to enforce it, who may be: (A) a marshal; (B) someone under contract with the United States; (C) someone specially appointed by the court for that purpose; or, (D) in an action brought by the United States, any officer or employee of the United States.

(c) Deposit in Court. If the property that is the subject of the action consists in whole or in part of freight, the proceeds of property sold, or other intangible property, the clerk must issue—in addition to the warrant—a summons directing any person controlling the property to show cause why it should not be deposited in court to abide the judgment.

(d) Supplemental Process. The clerk may upon application issue supplemental process to enforce the court's order without further court order.

(4) Notice. No notice other than execution of process is required when the property that is the subject of the action has been released under Rule E(5). If the property is not released within 10 days after execution, the plaintiff must promptly—or within the time that the court allows—give public notice of the action and arrest in a newspaper designated by court order and having general circulation in the district, but publication may be terminated if the property is released before publication is completed. The notice must specify the time under Rule C(6) to file a statement of interest in or right against the seized property and to answer. This rule does not affect the notice requirements in an action to foreclose a preferred ship mortgage under 46 U.S.C. §§ 31301 et seq., as amended.

(5) Ancillary Process. In any action in rem in which process has been served as provided by this rule, if any part of the property that is the subject of the action has not been brought within the control of the court because it has been removed or sold, or because it is intangible property in the hands of a person who has not been served with process, the court may, on motion, order any person having possession or control of such property or its proceeds to show cause why it should not be delivered into the custody of the marshal or other person or organization having a warrant for the arrest of the property, or paid into court to abide the judgment; and, after hearing, the court may enter such judgment as law and justice may require.

(6) Responsive Pleading; Interrogatories.

(a) Maritime Arrests and Other Proceedings.

(i) [A] person who asserts a right of possession or any ownership interest in the property that is the subject of the action must file a verified statement of right or interest:

(A) within 10 days after the execution of process, or

(B) within the time that the court allows;

(ii) the statement of right or interest must describe the interest in the property that supports the person's demand for its restitution or right to defend the action;

(iii) an agent, bailee, or attorney must state the authority to file a statement of right or interest on behalf of another; and

(iv) a person who asserts a right of possession or any ownership interest must serve an answer within 20 days after filing the statement of interest or right.

(b) Interrogatories. Interrogatories may be served with the complaint in an in rem action without leave of court. Answers to the interrogatories must be served with the answer to the complaint.

Rule D. Possessory, Petitory, and Partition Actions.

In all actions for possession, partition, and to try title maintainable according to the course of the admiralty practice with respect to a vessel, in all actions so maintainable with respect to the possession of cargo or other maritime property, and in all actions by one or more part owners against the others to obtain security for the return of the vessel from any voyage undertaken without their consent, or by one or more part owners against the others to obtain possession of the vessel for any voyage on giving security for its safe return, the process shall be by a warrant of arrest of the vessel, cargo, or other property, and by notice in the manner provided by Rule B(2) to the adverse party or parties.

Rule E. Actions in Rem and Quasi in Rem: General Provisions

(1) Applicability. Except as otherwise provided, this rule applies to actions in personam with process of maritime attachment and garnishment, actions in rem, and petitory, possessory, and partition actions, supplementing Rules B, C, and D.

(2) Complaint; Security.

(a) Complaint. In actions to which this rule is applicable the complaint shall state the circumstances from which the claim arises with such particularity that the defendant or claimant will be able, without moving for a more definite statement, to commence an investigation of the facts and to frame a responsive pleading.

(b) Security for Costs. Subject to the provisions of Rule 54(d) and of relevant statutes, the court may, on the filing of the complaint or on the appearance of any defendant, claimant, or any other party, or at any later time, require the plaintiff, defendant, claimant, or other party to give security, or additional security, in such sum as the court shall direct to pay all costs and expenses that shall be awarded against the party by any interlocutory order or by the final judgment, or on appeal by any appellate court.

(3) Process.

(a) In admiralty and maritime proceedings process in rem or of maritime attachment and garnishment may be served only within the district.

(b) Issuance and Delivery. Issuance and delivery of process in rem, or of maritime attachment and garnishment, shall be held in abeyance if the plaintiff so requests.

(4) Execution of Process; Marshal's Return; Custody of Property; Procedures for Release.

(a) In General. Upon issuance and delivery of the process, or, in the case of summons with process of attachment and garnishment, when it appears that the defendant cannot be found within the district, the marshal or other person or organization having a warrant shall forthwith execute the process in accordance with this subdivision (4), making due and prompt return.

(b) Tangible Property. If tangible property is to be attached or arrested, the marshal or other person or organization having the warrant shall take it into the marshal's possession for safe custody. If the character or situation of the property is such that the taking of actual possession is impracticable, the marshal or other person executing the process shall affix a copy thereof to the property in a conspicuous place and leave a copy of the complaint and process with the person having possession or the person's agent. In furtherance of the marshal's custody of any vessel the marshal is authorized to make a written request to the collector of customs not to grant clearance to such vessel until notified by the marshal or deputy marshal or by the clerk that the vessel has been released in accordance with these rules.

(c) Intangible Property. If intangible property is to be attached or arrested the marshal or other person or organization having the warrant shall execute the process by leaving with the garnishee or other obligor a copy of the complaint and process requiring the garnishee or other obligor to answer as provided in Rules B(3)(a) and C(6); or the marshal may accept for payment into the registry of the court the amount owed to the extent of the amount claimed by the plaintiff with interest and costs, in which event the garnishee or other obligor shall not be required to answer unless alias process shall be served.

* * *

(f) Procedure for Release From Arrest or Attachment. Whenever property is arrested or attached, any person claiming an interest in it shall be entitled to a prompt hearing at which the plaintiff shall be required to show why the arrest or attachment should not be vacated or other relief granted consistent with these rules. * * *

(5) Release of Property.

(a) Special Bond. Whenever process of maritime attachment and garnishment or process in rem is issued the execution of such process shall be stayed, or the property released, on the giving of security, to be approved by the court or clerk, or by stipulation of the parties, conditioned to answer the judgment of the court or of any appellate court. The parties may stipulate the amount and nature of such security. In the event of the inability or refusal of the parties so to stipulate the court shall fix the principal sum of the bond or stipulation at an amount sufficient to cover the amount of the plaintiff's claim fairly stated with accrued interest and costs; but the principal sum shall in no event exceed (i) twice the amount of the plaintiff's claim or (ii) the value of the property on due appraisement, whichever is smaller. The bond or stipulation shall be conditioned for the payment of the principal sum and interest thereon at 6 per cent per annum.

(b) General Bond. The owner of any vessel may file a general bond or stipulation, with sufficient surety, to be approved by the court, conditioned to answer the judgment of such court in all or any actions that may be brought thereafter in such court in which the vessel is attached or arrested. Thereupon the execution of all such process against such vessel shall be stayed so long as the amount secured by such bond or stipulation is at least double the aggregate amount claimed by plaintiffs in all actions begun and pending in which such vessel has been attached or arrested. Judgments and remedies may be had on such bond or stipulation as if a special bond or stipulation had been filed in each of such actions. The district court may make necessary orders to carry this rule into effect, particularly as to the giving of proper notice of any action against or attachment of a vessel for which a general bond has been filed. Such bond or stipulation shall be indorsed by the clerk with a minute of the actions wherein process is so stayed. Further security may be required by the court at any time.

If a special bond or stipulation is given in a particular case, the liability on the general bond or stipulation shall cease as to that case.

(c) Release by Consent or Stipulation; Order of Court or Clerk; Costs. Any vessel, cargo, or other property in the custody of the marshal or other person or organization having the warrant may be released forthwith upon the marshal's acceptance and approval of a stipulation, bond, or other security, signed by the party on whose behalf the property is detained or the party's attorney and expressly authorizing such release, if all costs and charges of the court and its officers shall have first been paid. Otherwise no property in the custody of the marshal, other person or organization having the warrant, or other officer of the court shall be released without an order of the court; but such order may be entered as of course by the clerk, upon the giving of approved security as provided by law and these rules, or upon the dismissal or discontinuance of the action; but the marshal or other person or organization having the warrant shall not deliver any property so released until the costs and charges of the officers of the court shall first have been paid.

(d) POSSESSORY, PETITORY, AND PARTITION ACTIONS. The foregoing provisions of this subdivision (5) do not apply to petitory, possessory, and partition actions. In such cases the property arrested shall be released only by order of the court, on such terms and conditions and on the giving of such security as the court may require.

(6) REDUCTION OR IMPAIRMENT OF SECURITY. Whenever security is taken the court may, on motion and hearing, for good cause shown, reduce the amount of security given; and if the surety shall be or become insufficient, new or additional sureties may be required on motion and hearing.

(7) SECURITY ON COUNTERCLAIM.

(a) When a person who has given security for damages in the original action asserts a counterclaim that arises from the transaction or occurrence that is the subject of the original action, a plaintiff for whose benefit the security has been given must give security for damages demanded in the counterclaim unless the court for cause shown, directs otherwise. Proceedings on the original claim must be stayed until this security is given unless the court directs otherwise.

(b) The plaintiff is required to give security under Rule E(7)(a) when the United States or its corporate instrumentality counterclaims and would have been required to give security to respond in damages if a private party but is relieved by law from giving security.

(8) RESTRICTED APPEARANCE. An appearance to defend against an admiralty and maritime claim with respect to which there has issued process in rem, or process of attachment and garnishment, may be expressly restricted to the defense of such claim, and in that event is not an appearance for the purposes of any other claim with respect to which such process is not available or has not been served.

(9) DISPOSITION OF PROPERTY; SALES.

(a) INTERLOCUTORY SALES; DELIVERY.

(i) On application of a party, the marshal, or other person having custody of the property, the court may order all or part of the property sold—with the sales proceeds, or as much of them as will satisfy the judgment, paid into court to await further orders of the court—if:

(A) the attached or arrested property is perishable, or liable to deterioration, decay, or injury by being detained in custody pending the action;

(B) the expense of keeping the property is excessive or disproportionate; or

(C) there is an unreasonable delay in securing release of the property.

(ii) In the circumstances described in Rule E(9)(a)(i), the court, on motion by a defendant or a person filing a statement of interest or right under Rule C(6), may order that the property, rather than being sold, be delivered to the movant upon giving security under these rules.

(b) SALES, PROCEEDS. All sales of property shall be made by the marshal or a deputy marshal, or by other person or organization having the warrant, or by any other person assigned by the court where the marshal or other person or organization having the warrant is a party in interest; and the proceeds of sale shall be forthwith paid into the registry of the court to be disposed of according to law.

(10) Preservation of Property. When the owner or another person remains in possession of property attached or arrested under the provisions of Rule E(4)(b) that permit execution of process without taking actual possession, the court, on a party's motion or on its own, may enter any order necessary to preserve the property and to prevent its removal.

Rule F. Limitation of Liability.

(1) Time for Filing Complaint; Security. Not later than six months after receipt of a claim in writing, any vessel owner may file a complaint in the appropriate district court, as provided in subdivision (9) of this rule, for limitation of liability pursuant to statute. The owner (a) shall deposit with the court, for the benefit of claimants, a sum equal to the amount or value of the owner's interest in the vessel and pending freight, or approved security therefor, and in addition such sums, or approved security therefor, as the court may from time to time fix as necessary to carry out the provisions of the statutes as amended; or (b) at the owner's option shall transfer to a trustee to be appointed by the court, for the benefit of claimants, the owner's interest in the vessel and pending freight, together with such sums, or approved security therefor, as the court may from time to time fix as necessary to carry out the provisions of the statutes as amended. The plaintiff shall also give security for costs and, if the plaintiff elects to give security, for interest at the rate of 6 percent per annum from the date of the security.

(2) Complaint. The complaint shall set forth the facts on the basis of which the right to limit liability is asserted and all facts necessary to enable the court to determine the amount to which the owner's liability shall be limited. The complaint may demand exoneration from as well as limitation of liability. It shall state the voyage if any, on which the demands sought to be limited arose, with the date and place of its termination; the amount of all demands including all unsatisfied liens or claims of lien, in contract or in tort or otherwise, arising on that voyage, so far as known to the plaintiff, and what actions and proceedings, if any, are pending thereon; whether the vessel was damaged, lost, or abandoned, and, if so, when and where; the value of the vessel at the close of the voyage or, in case of wreck, the value of her wreckage, strippings, or proceeds, if any, and where and in whose possession they are; and the amount of any pending freight recovered or recoverable. If the plaintiff elects to transfer the plaintiff's interest in the vessel to a trustee, the complaint must further show any prior paramount liens thereon, and what voyages or trips, if any, she has made since the voyage or trip on which the claims sought to be limited arose, and any existing liens arising upon any such subsequent voyage or trip, with the amounts and causes thereof, and the names and addresses of the lienors, so far as known; and whether the vessel sustained any injury upon or by reason of such subsequent voyage or trip.

(3) Claims Against Owner; Injunction. Upon compliance by the owner with the requirements of subdivision (1) of this rule all claims and proceedings against the owner or the owner's property with respect to the matter in question shall cease. On application of the plaintiff the court shall enjoin the further prosecution of any action or proceeding against the plaintiff or the plaintiff's property with respect to any claim subject to limitation in the action.

(4) Notice to Claimants. Upon the owner's compliance with subdivision (1) of this rule the court shall issue a notice to all persons asserting claims with respect to which the complaint seeks limitation, admonishing them to file their respective claims with the clerk of the court and to serve on the attorneys for the plaintiff a copy thereof on or before a date to be named in the notice. The date so fixed shall not be less than 30 days after is-

suance of the notice. For cause shown, the court may enlarge the time within which claims may be filed. The notice shall be published in such newspaper or newspapers as the court may direct once a week for four successive weeks prior to the date fixed for the filing of claims. The plaintiff not later than the day of second publication shall also mail a copy of the notice to every person known to have made any claim against the vessel or the plaintiff arising out of the voyage or trip on which the claims sought to be limited arose. In cases involving death a copy of such notice shall be mailed to the decedent at the decedent's last known address, and also to any person who shall be known to have made any claim on account of such death.

(5) CLAIMS AND ANSWER. Claims shall be filed and served on or before the date specified in the notice provided for in subdivision (4) of this rule. Each claim shall specify the facts upon which the claimant relies in support of the claim, the items thereof, and the dates on which the same accrued. If a claimant desires to contest either the right to exoneration from or the right to limitation of liability the claimant shall file and serve an answer to the complaint unless the claim has included an answer.

(6) INFORMATION TO BE GIVEN CLAIMANTS. Within 30 days after the date specified in the notice for filing claims, or within such time as the court thereafter may allow, the plaintiff shall mail to the attorney for each claimant (or if the claimant has no attorney to the claimant) a list setting forth (a) the name of each claimant, (b) the name and address of the claimant's attorney (if the claimant is known to have one), (c) the nature of the claim, i.e., whether property loss, property damage, death, personal injury etc., and (d) the amount thereof.

(7) INSUFFICIENCY OF FUND OR SECURITY. Any claimant may by motion demand that the funds deposited in court or the security given by the plaintiff be increased on the ground that they are less than the value of the plaintiff's interest in the vessel and pending freight. Thereupon the court shall cause due appraisement to be made of the value of the plaintiff's interest in the vessel and pending freight; and if the court finds that the deposit or security is either insufficient or excessive it shall order its increase or reduction. In like manner any claimant may demand that the deposit or security be increased on the ground that it is insufficient to carry out the provisions of the statutes relating to claims in respect of loss of life or bodily injury; and, after notice and hearing, the court may similarly order that the deposit or security be increased or reduced.

(8) OBJECTIONS TO CLAIMS: DISTRIBUTION OF FUND. Any interested party may question or controvert any claim without filing an objection thereto. Upon determination of liability the fund deposited or secured, or the proceeds of the vessel and pending freight, shall be divided pro rata, subject to all relevant provisions of law, among the several claimants in proportion to the amounts of their respective claims, duly proved, saving, however, to all parties any priority to which they may be legally entitled.

(9) VENUE; TRANSFER. The complaint shall be filed in any district in which the vessel has been attached or arrested to answer for any claim with respect to which the plaintiff seeks to limit liability; or, if the vessel has not been attached or arrested, then in any district in which the owner has been sued with respect to any such claim. When the vessel has not been attached or arrested to answer the matters aforesaid, and suit has not been commenced against the owner, the proceedings may be had in the district in which the vessel may be, but if the vessel is not within any district and no suit has been commenced in any district, then the complaint may be filed in any district. For the convenience of parties and witnesses, in the interest of justice, the court may transfer the action to any district; if venue is wrongly laid the court shall dismiss or, if it be in the interest of jus-

tice, transfer the action to any district in which it could have been brought. If the vessel shall have been sold, the proceeds shall represent the vessel for the purposes of these rules.

The Rules Prior to the 2007 "Plain-English" Amendments

FED. R. CIV. P. 4(k). TERRITORIAL LIMITS OF EFFECTIVE SERVICE.

(1) Service of a summons or filing a waiver of service is effective to establish jurisdiction over the person of a defendant

(A) who could be subjected to the jurisdiction of a court of general jurisdiction in the state in which the district court is located, or

(B) who is a party joined under Rule 14 or Rule 19 and is served at a place within a judicial district of the United States and not more than 100 miles from the place from which the summons issues, or

(C) who is subject to the federal interpleader jurisdiction under 28 U.S.C. § 1335, or

(D) when authorized by a statute of the United States.

(2) If the exercise of jurisdiction is consistent with the Constitution and laws of the United States, serving a summons or filing a waiver of service is also effective, with respect to claims arising under federal law, to establish personal jurisdiction over the person of any defendant who is not subject to the jurisdiction of the courts of general jurisdiction of any state.

FED. R. CIV. P. 9(h). ADMIRALTY AND MARITIME CLAIMS.

A pleading or count setting forth a claim for relief within the admiralty and maritime jurisdiction that is also within the jurisdiction of the district court on some other ground may contain a statement identifying the claim as an admiralty or maritime claim for the purposes of Rules 14(c), 38(e), 82, and the Supplemental Rules for Admiralty or Maritime Claims and Asset Forfeiture Actions. If the claim is cognizable only in admiralty, it is an admiralty or maritime claim for those purposes whether so identified or not. The amendment of a pleading to add or withdraw an identifying statement is governed by the principles of Rule 15. A case that includes an admiralty or maritime claim within this subdivision is an admiralty case within 28 U.S.C. § 1292(a)(3).

FED. R. CIV. P. 14. THIRD-PARTY PRACTICE.

(a) WHEN DEFENDANT MAY BRING IN THIRD PARTY. At any time after commencement of the action a defending party, as a third-party plaintiff, may cause a summons and complaint to be served upon a person not a party to the action who is or may be liable to the third-party plaintiff for all or part of the plaintiff's claim against the third-party plaintiff. * * *

* * *

(c) ADMIRALTY AND MARITIME CLAIMS. When a plaintiff asserts an admiralty or maritime claim within the meaning of Rule 9(h), the defendant or person who asserts a right under Supplemental Rule C(6)(a)(i), as a third-party plaintiff, may bring in a third-party defendant who may be wholly or partly liable, either to the plaintiff or to the third-party plaintiff, by way of remedy over, contribution, or otherwise on account of the same transaction, occurrence, or series of transactions or occurrences. In such a case the third-party plaintiff may also demand judgment against the third-party defendant in favor of the plaintiff, in which event the third-party defendant shall make any defenses to the claim of the plaintiff as well as to that of the third-party plaintiff in the manner provided in Rule 12 and the action shall proceed as if the plaintiff had commenced it against the third-party defendant as well as the third-party plaintiff.

FED. R. CIV. P. 38. JURY TRIAL OF RIGHT.

(a) RIGHT PRESERVED. The right of trial by jury as declared by the Seventh Amendment to the Constitution or as given by a statute of the United States shall be preserved to the parties inviolate.

* * *

(e) ADMIRALTY AND MARITIME CLAIMS. These rules shall not be construed to create a right to trial by jury of the issues in an admiralty or maritime claim within the meaning of Rule 9(h).

FED. R. CIV. P. 82. JURISDICTION AND VENUE UNAFFECTED.

These rules shall not be construed to extend or limit the jurisdiction of the United States district courts or the venue of actions therein. An admiralty or maritime claim within the meaning of Rule 9(h) shall not be treated as a civil action for the purposes of [28 U.S.C. §§ 1391–92].

[The Supplemental Rules for Certain Admiralty and Maritime Claims were not affected by the 2007 "Plain-English" Amendments.]

International Material

1910 Brussels Convention for the Unification of Certain Rules of Law with Respect to Collision between Vessels

The 1910 Collision Convention entered into force in 1913. It is not in force in the United States, apparently because U.S. cargo interests objected to the lack of joint and several liability in the second paragraph of Article 4. Selected provisions of the Convention are reproduced here.

Article 1

Where a collision occurs between sea-going vessels or between sea-going vessels and vessels of inland navigation, the compensation due for damages caused to the vessels, or to any things or persons on board thereof, shall be settled in accordance with the following provisions, in whatever waters the collision takes place.

Article 2

If the collision * * * is caused by *force majeure*, or if the causes of the collision are left in doubt, the damages are borne by those who have suffered them.

This provision shall be applicable notwithstanding the fact that the vessels, or any one of them, may be at anchor (or otherwise made fast) at the time of the casualty.

Article 3

If the collision is caused by the fault of one of the vessels, liability to make good the damages shall attach to the one which has committed the fault.

Article 4

If two or more vessels are in fault the liability of each vessel shall be in proportion to the degree of the faults respectively committed. Provided that if, having regard to the circumstances, it is not possible to establish the degree of the respective faults, or if it appears that the faults are equal, the liability shall be apportioned equally.

The damages caused either to the vessels, or to their cargoes, or to the effects or other property of the crews, passengers, or other persons on board, shall be borne by the vessels in fault in the above proportion without joint and several liability toward third parties.

In respect of damages caused by death or personal injury, the vessels in fault shall be jointly as well as severally liable to third parties, without prejudice to the right of recourse of the vessel which has paid a larger part than that which in accordance with the provisions of the first paragraph of this article she ought ultimately to bear.

It is left to the law of each country to determine, as regards such recourse, the scope and effect of any legal or contractual provisions which limit the liability of the owners of a vessel toward persons on board.

Article 5 ·

The liability imposed by the preceding Articles shall attach, in cases where the collision is caused by the fault of a pilot, even when the carrying of the pilot is obligatory.

Article 8

After a collision, the master of each of the vessels in collision shall be bound, so far as he can do so without serious danger to his vessel, her crew, and her passengers, to render assistance to the other vessel, her crew, and her passengers.

* * *

Article 11

This Convention shall not apply to ships of war or to Government ships appropriated exclusively to a public service.

International Regulations for Preventing Collisions at Sea, 1972 (COLREGS)

The first diplomatic conference on navigational rules was held in Washington in 1889. The resulting rules became effective throughout the world in 1897. The current navigational rules, which became effective in 1977, were adopted at a 1972 diplomatic conference in London under the auspices of the United Nations agency now known as the International Maritime Organization (IMO). Minor amendments, primarily technical in nature, became effective in 1983, 1989, 1991, and 2003. In the United States, the official source for each amendment is the relevant presidential proclamation published in the Federal Register. The most convenient source for the amended COLREGS is an unofficial reprint in a secondary source, such as volume 6 of Benedict on Admiralty.

Prior to 1981, the United States had three separate sets of rules to govern inland navigation: the Inland Rules, the Western Rivers Rules, and the Great Lakes Rules. Since 1981, uniform Inland Rules, which are similar or identical to COLREGS in most respects, apply on all U.S. waters not governed by COLREGS. For many years, the Inland Rules have been codified at 33 U.S.C. §§ 2001–38. In 2004, Congress repealed the codified rules as of the "effective date of final regulations prescribed by the Secretary of the Department in which the Coast Guard is operating," currently the Department of Homeland Security. Under 33 U.S.C. § 2071, these new inland navigation regulations are to be "as consistent as possible" with COLREGS. (At this writing, the Inland Rules at 33 U.S.C. §§ 2001–38 remain in force. It may take the Coast Guard some time to finish the new ones.)

Rule 1. Application

(a) These Rules shall apply to all vessels upon the high seas and in all waters connected therewith navigable by seagoing vessels.

* * *

Rule 2. Responsibility

(a) Nothing in these Rules shall exonerate any vessel, or the owner, master or crew thereof, from the consequences of any neglect to comply with these Rules or of the neglect of any precaution which may be required by the ordinary practice of seamen, or by the special circumstances of the case.

(b) In construing and complying with these Rules due regard shall be had to all dangers of navigation and collision and to any special circumstances, including the limitations of the vessels involved, which may make a departure from these Rules necessary to avoid immediate danger.

Rule 4. Application

Rules in this section[1] apply in any condition of visibility.

Rule 5. Look-out

Every vessel shall at all times maintain a proper look-out by sight and hearing as well as by all available means appropriate in the prevailing circumstances and conditions so as to make a full appraisal of the situation and of the risk of collision.

---

1. Editors' note: The reference is to section I of Part B, which includes Rules 4–10.

Rule 6. Safe Speed

Every vessel shall at all times proceed at a safe speed so that she can take proper and effective action to avoid collision and be stopped within a distance appropriate to the prevailing circumstances and conditions. In determining a safe speed the following factors shall be among those taken into account:

(a) By all vessels:

(i) the state of visibility.

(ii) the traffic density including concentrations of fishing vessels or any other vessels;

(iii) the manoeuvrability of the vessel with special reference to stopping distance and turning ability in the prevailing conditions;

(iv) at night the presence of background light such as from shore lights or from back scatter of her own lights;

(v) the state of wind, sea and current, and the proximity of navigational hazards;

(vi) the draught in relation to the available depth of water.

(b) Additionally, by vessels with operational radar:

(i) the characteristics, efficiency and limitations of the radar equipment;

(ii) any constraints imposed by the radar range scale in use;

(iii) the effect on radar detection of the sea state, weather and other sources of interference;

(iv) the possibility that small vessels, ice and other floating objects may not be detected by radar at an adequate range;

(v) the number, location and movement of vessels detected by radar;

(vi) the more exact assessment of the visibility that may be possible when radar is used to determine the range of vessels or other objects in the vicinity.

Rule 7. Risk of Collision

(a) Every vessel shall use all available means appropriate to the prevailing circumstances and conditions to determine if risk of collision exists. If there is any doubt such risk shall be deemed to exist.

(b) Proper use shall be made of radar equipment if fitted and operational, including long-range scanning to obtain early warning of risk of collision and radar plotting or equivalent systematic observation of detected objects.

* * *

Rule 8. Action to Avoid Collision

(a) Any action to avoid collision shall be taken in accordance with the Rules of this Part[2] and shall, if the circumstances of the case admit, be positive, made in ample time and with due regard to the observance of good seamanship.

(b) Any alteration of course and/or speed to avoid collision shall, if the circumstances of the case admit, be large enough to be readily apparent to another vessel observing visually or by radar; a succession of small alterations of course and/or speed should be avoided.

---

2. Editors' note: The reference is to Part B, which includes Rules 4–19.

(c) If there is sufficient sea room, alteration of course alone may be the most effective action to avoid a close-quarters situation provided that it is made in good time, is substantial and does not result in another close-quarters situation.

(d) Action taken to avoid collision with another vessel shall be such as to result in passing at a safe distance. The effectiveness of the action shall be carefully checked until the other vessel is finally past and clear.

(e) If necessary to avoid collision or allow more time to assess the situation, a vessel shall slacken her speed or take all way off by stopping or reversing her means of propulsion.

(f) (i) A vessel which, by any of these Rules, is required not to impede the passage or safe passage of another vessel shall, when required by the circumstances of the case, take early action to allow sufficient sea room for the safe passage of the other vessel.

(ii) A vessel required not to impede the passage or safe passage of another vessel is not relieved of this obligation if approaching the other vessel so as to involve risk of collision and shall, when taking action, have full regard to the action which may be required by the Rules of this part.

(iii) A vessel the passage of which is not to be impeded remains fully obliged to comply with the Rules of this part when the two vessels are approaching one another so as to involve risk of collision.

Rule 10. Traffic Separation Schemes

(a) This Rule applies to traffic separation schemes adopted by the [International Maritime] Organization and does not relieve any vessel of her obligation under any other rule.

(b) A vessel using a traffic separation scheme shall:

(i) proceed in the appropriate traffic lane in the general direction of traffic flow for that lane;

(ii) so far as practicable keep clear of a traffic separation line or separation zone;

(iii) normally join or leave a traffic lane at the termination of the lane, but when joining or leaving from either side shall do so at as small an angle to the general direction of traffic flow as practicable.

(c) A vessel shall, so far as practicable, avoid crossing traffic lanes but if obliged to do so shall cross on a heading as nearly as practicable at right angles to the general direction of traffic flow.

(d) (i) A vessel shall not use an inshore traffic zone when she can safely use the appropriate traffic lane within the adjacent traffic separation scheme. However, vessels of less than 20 metres in length, sailing vessels and vessels engaged in fishing may use the inshore traffic zone.

(ii) Notwithstanding subparagraph (d)(i), a vessel may use an inshore traffic zone when en route to or from a port, offshore installation or structure, pilot station or any other place situated within the inshore traffic zone, or to avoid immediate danger.

(e) A vessel other than a crossing vessel or a vessel joining or leaving a lane shall not normally enter a separation zone or cross a separation line except:

(i) in cases of emergency to avoid immediate danger;

(ii) to engage in fishing within a separation zone.

(f) A vessel navigating in areas near the terminations of traffic separation schemes shall do so with particular caution.

(g) A vessel shall so far as practicable avoid anchoring in a traffic separation scheme or in areas near its terminations

(h) A vessel not using a traffic separation scheme shall avoid it by as wide a margin as is practicable.

(i) A vessel engaged in fishing shall not impede the passage of any vessel following a traffic lane.

(j) A vessel of less than 20 metres in length or a sailing vessel shall not impede the safe passage of a power-driven vessel following a traffic lane.

(k) A vessel restricted in her ability to manoeuvre when engaged in an operation for the maintenance of safety of navigation in a traffic separation scheme is exempted from complying with this Rule to the extent necessary to carry out the operation.

(l) A vessel restricted in her ability to manoeuvre when engaged in an operation for the laying, servicing or picking up of a submarine cable, within a traffic separation scheme, is exempted from complying with this Rule to the extent necessary to carry out the operation.

Rule 11. Application

Rules in this section[3] apply to vessels in sight of one another.

Rule 13. Overtaking

(a) Notwithstanding anything contained in the Rules of part B, sections I and II,[4] any vessel overtaking any other shall keep out of the way of the vessel being overtaken.

(b) A vessel shall be deemed to be overtaking when coming up with another vessel from a direction more than 22.5 degrees abaft her beam, that is, in such a position with reference to the vessel she is overtaking, that at night she would be able to see only the sternlight of that vessel but neither of her sidelights.

(c) When a vessel is in any doubt as to whether she is overtaking another, she shall assume that this is the case and act accordingly.

(d) Any subsequent alteration of the bearing between the two vessels shall not make the overtaking vessel a crossing vessel within the meaning of these Rules or relieve her of the duty of keeping clear of the overtaken vessel until she is finally past and clear.

Rule 14. Head-on Situation

(a) When two power-driven vessels are meeting on reciprocal or nearly reciprocal courses so as to involve risk of collision each shall alter her course to starboard so that each shall pass on the port side of the other.

(b) Such a situation shall be deemed to exist when a vessel sees the other ahead or nearly ahead and by night she could see the masthead lights of the other in a line or nearly in a line and/or both sidelights and by day she observes the corresponding aspect of the other vessel.

(c) When a vessel is in any doubt as to whether such a situation exists she shall assume that it does exist and act accordingly.

---

3. Editors' note: The reference is to section II of Part B, which includes Rules 11–18.
4. Editors' note: The reference includes Rules 4–18.

Rule 15. Crossing situation

When two power-driven vessels are crossing so as to involve risk of collision, the vessel which has the other on her own starboard side shall keep out of the way and shall, if the circumstances of the case admit, avoid crossing ahead of the other vessel.

Rule 16. Action by give-way vessel

Every vessel which is directed to keep out of the way of another vessel shall, so far as possible, take early and substantial action to keep well clear.

Rule 17. Action by Stand-on Vessel

(a) (i) Where one of two vessels is to keep out of the way the other shall keep her course and speed.

(ii) The latter vessel may however take action to avoid collision by her manoeuvre alone, as soon as it becomes apparent to her that the vessel required to keep out of the way is not taking appropriate action in compliance with these Rules.

(b) When, from any cause, the vessel required to keep her course and speed finds herself so close that collision cannot be avoided by the action of the give-way vessel alone, she shall take such action as will best aid to avoid collision.

(c) A power-driven vessel which takes action in a crossing situation in accordance with subparagraph (a)(ii) of this Rule to avoid collision with another power-driven vessel shall, if the circumstances of the case admit, not alter course to port for a vessel on her own port side.

(d) This Rule does not relieve the give-way vessel of her obligation to keep out of the way.

Rule 19. Conduct of vessels in restricted visibility

(a) This Rule applies to vessels not in sight of one another when navigating in or near an area of restricted visibility.

(b) Every vessel shall proceed at a safe speed adapted to the prevailing circumstances and conditions of restricted visibility. A power-driven vessel shall have her engines ready for immediate manoeuvre.

(c) Every vessel shall have due regard to the prevailing circumstances and conditions of restricted visibility when complying with the Rules of section I of this part.[5]

(d) A vessel which detects by radar alone the presence of another vessel shall determine if a close-quarters situation is developing and/or risk of collision exists. If so, she shall take avoiding action in ample time, provided that when such action consists of an alteration of course, so far as possible the following shall be avoided:

(i) an alteration of course to port for a vessel forward of the beam, other than for a vessel being overtaken;

(ii) an alteration of course towards a vessel abeam or abaft the beam.

(e) Except where it has been determined that a risk of collision does not exist, every vessel which hears apparently forward of her beam the fog signal of another vessel, or which cannot avoid a close-quarters situation with another vessel forward of her beam, shall reduce her speed to the minimum at which she can be kept on her course. She shall if necessary take all her way off and in any event navigate with extreme caution until danger of collision is over.

---

5. Editors' note: The reference is to section I of Part B, which includes Rules 4–10.

York-Antwerp Rules 2004

One of the earliest efforts to achieve widespread legal uniformity through international agreement was on the subject of general average. The York Rules governing general average were adopted at a conference in York in 1864. These were revised at a conference in Antwerp in 1877 to produce the first set of York-Antwerp Rules. Since then, the Rules have generally been revised every 20–25 years. Since World War II, these revisions have been under the auspices of the Comité Maritime International (CMI). The Rules now consist of a Rule of Interpretation, a Rule Paramount, seven lettered Rules (A–G), and twenty-three numbered Rules (I–XXIII).

Unlike most of the materials in this Supplement, the York-Antwerp Rules gain their legal force solely through voluntary incorporation into private contracts. They have never been adopted by an international convention, and are rarely enacted as domestic legislation. But they are so widely accepted by private agreement that they provide the governing rules in virtually all general average disputes.

Rule of Interpretation

In the adjustment of general average the following Rules shall apply to the exclusion of any Law and Practice inconsistent therewith.

Except as provided by the Rule Paramount and the numbered Rules, general average shall be adjusted according to the lettered Rules.

Rule Paramount

In no case shall there be any allowance for sacrifice or expenditure unless reasonably made or incurred.

Rule A

1.   There is a general average act when, and only when, any extraordinary sacrifice or expenditure is intentionally and reasonably made or incurred for the common safety for the purpose of preserving from peril the property involved in a common maritime adventure.

2.   General average sacrifices and expenditures shall be borne by the different contributing interests on the basis hereinafter provided.

Rule B

1.   There is a common maritime adventure when one or more vessels are towing or pushing another vessel or vessels, provided that they are all involved in commercial activities and not in a salvage operation.

When measures are taken to preserve the vessels and their cargoes, if any, from a common peril, these Rules shall apply.

2.   A vessel is not in common peril with another vessel or vessels if by simply disconnecting from the other vessel or vessels she is in safety; but if the disconnection is itself a general average act the common maritime adventure continues.

Rule C

1.   Only such losses, damages or expenses which are the direct consequence of the general average act shall be allowed as general average.

2.   In no case shall there be any allowance in general average for losses, damages or expenses incurred in respect of damage to the environment or in consequence of the es-

cape or release of pollutant substances from the property involved in the common maritime adventure.

3.   Demurrage, loss of market, and any loss or damage sustained or expense incurred by reason of delay, whether on the voyage or subsequently, and any indirect loss whatsoever, shall not be allowed as general average.

Rule D

Rights to contribution in general average shall not be affected, though the event which gave rise to the sacrifice or expenditure may have been due to the fault of one of the parties to the adventure, but this shall not prejudice any remedies or defences which may be open against or to that party in respect of such fault.

Rule E

1.   The onus of proof is upon the party claiming in general average to show that the loss or expense claimed is properly allowable as general average.

* * *

Rule F

Any additional expense incurred in place of another expense, which would have been allowable as general average shall be deemed to be general average and so allowed without regard to the saving, if any, to other interests, but only up to the amount of the general average expense avoided.

Rule G

1.   General average shall be adjusted as regards both loss and contribution upon the basis of values at the time and place when and where the adventure ends.

* * *

Rule I — Jettison of Cargo

No jettison of cargo shall be allowed as general average, unless such cargo is carried in accordance with the recognised custom of the trade.

Rule II — Loss or Damage by Sacrifices for the Common Safety

Loss of or damage to the property involved in the common maritime adventure by or in consequence of a sacrifice made for the common safety, and by water which goes down a ship's hatches opened or other opening made for the purpose of making a jettison for the common safety, shall be allowed as general average.

Rule III — Extinguishing Fire on Shipboard

Damage done to a ship and cargo, or either of them, by water or otherwise, including damage by beaching or scuttling a burning ship, in extinguishing a fire on board the ship, shall be allowed as general average; except that no allowance shall be made for damage by smoke however caused or by heat of the fire.

Rule IV — Cutting Away Wreck

Loss or damage sustained by cutting away wreck or parts of the ship which have been previously carried away or are effectively lost by accident shall not be allowed as general average.

Rule V — Voluntary Stranding

When a ship is intentionally run on shore for the common safety, whether or not she might have been driven on shore, the consequent loss or damage to the property involved in the common maritime adventure shall be allowed in general average.

Rule VI — Salvage Remuneration

(a) Salvage payments, including interest thereon and legal fees associated with such payments, shall lie where they fall and shall not be allowed in general average, save only that if one party to the salvage shall have paid all or any of the proportion of salvage (including interest and legal fees) due from another party (calculated on the basis of salved values and not general average contributory values), the unpaid contribution to salvage due from that other party shall be credited in the adjustment to the party that has paid it, and debited to the party on whose behalf the payment was made.

(b) Salvage payments referred to in paragraph (a) above shall include any salvage remuneration in which the skill and efforts of the salvors in preventing or minimising damage to the environment such as is referred to in Article 13 paragraph 1(b) of the International Convention on Salvage 1989 have been taken into account.

* * *

Rule X — Expenses of Port of Refuge, etc.

(a) (i) When a ship shall have entered a port or place of refuge or shall have returned to her port or place of loading in consequence of accident, sacrifice or other extraordinary circumstances which render that necessary for the common safety, the expenses of entering such port or place shall be allowed as general average; and when she shall have sailed thence with her original cargo, or a part of it, the corresponding expenses of leaving such port or place consequent upon such entry or return shall likewise be allowed as general average.

* * *

(b) (i) The cost of handling on board or discharging cargo, fuel or stores whether at a port or place of loading, call or refuge, shall be allowed as general average, when the handling or discharge was necessary for the common safety or to enable damage to the ship caused by sacrifice or accident to be repaired, if the repairs were necessary for the safe prosecution of the voyage, except in cases where the damage to the ship is discovered at a port or place of loading or call without any accident or other extraordinary circumstances connected with such damage having taken place during the voyage.

* * *

Rule XI — Wages and Maintenance of Crew and other expenses putting in to and at a port of refuge, etc.

(a) Wages and maintenance of master, officers and crew reasonably incurred and fuel and stores consumed during the prolongation of the voyage occasioned by a ship entering a port or place of refuge or returning to her port or place of loading shall be allowed as general average when the expenses of entering such port or place are allowable as general average in accordance with Rule X(a).

(b) For the purpose of this and the other Rules wages shall include all payments made to or for the benefit of the master, officers and crew, whether such payments be imposed by law upon the shipowners or be made under the terms of articles of employment.

(c) (i) When a ship shall have entered or been detained in any port or place in consequence of accident, sacrifice or other extraordinary circumstances which render that necessary for the common safety, or to enable damage to the ship caused by sacrifice or accident to be repaired, if the repairs were necessary for the safe prosecution of the voyage, fuel and stores consumed during the extra period of detention in such port or place until the ship shall or should have been made ready to proceed upon her voyage, shall be allowed as general average, except such fuel and stores as are consumed in effecting repairs not allowable in general average.

(ii) Port charges incurred during the extra period of detention shall likewise be allowed as general average except such charges as are incurred solely by reason of repairs not allowable in general average.

(iii) Provided that when damage to the ship is discovered at a port or place of loading or call without any accident or other extraordinary circumstance connected with such damage having taken place during the voyage, then fuel and stores consumed and port charges incurred during the extra detention for repairs to damages so discovered shall not be allowable as general average, even if the repairs are necessary for the safe prosecution of the voyage.

(iv) When the ship is condemned or does not proceed on her original voyage, fuel and stores consumed and port charges shall be allowed as general average only up to the date of the ship's condemnation or of the abandonment of the voyage or up to the date of completion of discharge of cargo if the condemnation or abandonment takes place before that date.

* * *

Rule XII — Damage to Cargo in Discharging, etc.

Damage to or loss of cargo, fuel or stores sustained in consequence of their handling, discharging, storing, reloading and stowing shall be allowed as general average, when and only when the cost of those measures respectively is allowed as general average.

Rule XIII — Deduction from Cost of Repairs

(a) Repairs to be allowed in general average shall not be subject to deductions in respect of "new for old" where old material or parts are replaced by new unless the ship is over fifteen years old in which case there shall be a deduction of one third. * * *

Rule XIV — Temporary Repairs

(a) Where temporary repairs are effected to a ship at a port of loading, call or refuge, for the common safety, or of damage caused by general average sacrifice, the cost of such repairs shall be allowed as general average.

(b) Where temporary repairs of accidental damage are effected in order to enable the adventure to be completed, the cost of such repairs shall be allowed as general average without regard to the saving, if any, to other interests, but only up to the saving in expense which would have been incurred and allowed in general average if such repairs had not been effected there. Provided that for the purposes of this paragraph only, the cost of temporary repairs falling for consideration shall be limited to the extent that the cost of temporary repairs effected at the port of loading, call or refuge, together with either the cost of permanent repairs eventually effected or, if unrepaired at the time of the adjustment, the reasonable depreciation in the value of the vessel at the completion of the voyage exceeds the cost of permanent repairs had they been effected at the port of loading, call or refuge.

(c) No deductions "new for old" shall be made from the cost of temporary repairs allowable as general average.

Rule XV — Loss of Freight

Loss of freight arising from damage to or loss of cargo shall be allowed as general average, either when caused by a general average act, or when the damage to or loss of cargo is so allowed.

Deduction shall be made from the amount of gross freight lost, of the charges which the owner thereof would have incurred to earn such freight, but has, in consequence of the sacrifice, not incurred.

Proposed UNCITRAL Convention on Contracts for the International Carriage of Goods Wholly or Partly by Sea (the Rotterdam Rules)

As this Supplement goes to press, the United Nations Commission on International Trade Law (UNCITRAL) has just completed its work on a new multilateral convention to modernize the legal regime governing international transport law. See Casebook at 291 note 3. The proposed convention is scheduled for consideration by the General Assembly in October 2008. If the General Assembly approves, the new convention will be opened for signature at a ceremony in Rotterdam in September 2009.

When the convention enters into force, it will supersede the Carriage of Goods by Sea Act (supra at 67) in the United States. Internationally, it will supersede the Hague, Hague-Visby, and Hamburg Rules. See Casebook at 288–290. It will be popularly known as the Rotterdam Rules. Selected provisions are reproduced here. The full text and the latest news on its current status will be available on UNCITRAL's web site, www.uncitral.org.

CHAPTER 1. GENERAL PROVISIONS

Article 1. Definitions

For the purposes of this Convention:

1. "Contract of carriage" means a contract in which a carrier, against the payment of freight, undertakes to carry goods from one place to another. The contract shall provide for carriage by sea and may provide for carriage by other modes of transport in addition to the sea carriage.

2. "Volume contract" means a contract of carriage that provides for the carriage of a specified quantity of goods in a series of shipments during an agreed period of time. The specification of the quantity may include a minimum, a maximum or a certain range.

3. "Liner transportation" means a transportation service that is offered to the public through publication or similar means and includes transportation by ships operating on a regular schedule between specified ports in accordance with publicly available timetables of sailing dates.

4. "Non-liner transportation" means any transportation that is not liner transportation.

5. "Carrier" means a person that enters into a contract of carriage with a shipper.

6. (a) "Performing party" means a person other than the carrier that performs or undertakes to perform any of the carrier's obligations under a contract of carriage with respect to the receipt, loading, handling, stowage, carriage, care, unloading or delivery of the goods, to the extent that such person acts, either directly or indirectly, at the carrier's request or under the carrier's supervision or control.

(b) "Performing party" does not include any person that is retained, directly or indirectly, by a shipper, by a documentary shipper, by the controlling party or by the consignee instead of by the carrier.

7. "Maritime performing party" means a performing party to the extent that it performs or undertakes to perform any of the carrier's obligations during the period between the arrival of the goods at the port of loading of a ship and their departure from the port of

discharge of a ship. An inland carrier is a maritime performing party only if it performs or undertakes to perform its services exclusively within a port area.

8. "Shipper" means a person that enters into a contract of carriage with a carrier.

9. "Documentary shipper" means a person, other than the shipper, that accepts to be named as "shipper" in the transport document or electronic transport record.

* * *

14. "Transport document" means a document issued under a contract of carriage by the carrier that:

(a) Evidences the carrier's or a performing party's receipt of goods under a contract of carriage; and

(b) Evidences or contains a contract of carriage.

15. "Negotiable transport document" means a transport document that indicates, by wording such as "to order" or "negotiable" or other appropriate wording recognized as having the same effect by the law applicable to the document, that the goods have been consigned to the order of the shipper, to the order of the consignee, or to bearer, and is not explicitly stated as being "non-negotiable" or "not negotiable".

16. "Non-negotiable transport document" means a transport document that is not a negotiable transport document.

* * *

23. "Contract particulars" means any information relating to the contract of carriage or to the goods (including terms, notations, signatures and endorsements) that is in a transport document or an electronic transport record.

24. "Goods" means the wares, merchandise, and articles of every kind whatsoever that a carrier undertakes to carry under a contract of carriage and includes the packing and any equipment and container not supplied by or on behalf of the carrier.

25. "Ship" means any vessel used to carry goods by sea.

26. "Container" means any type of container, transportable tank or flat, swapbody, or any similar unit load used to consolidate goods, and any equipment ancillary to such unit load.

27. "Vehicle" means a road or railroad cargo vehicle.

28. "Freight" means the remuneration payable to the carrier for the carriage of goods under a contract of carriage.

29. "Domicile" means (a) a place where a company or other legal person or association of natural or legal persons has its (i) statutory seat or place of incorporation or central registered office, whichever is applicable, (ii) central administration or (iii) principal place of business, and (b) the habitual residence of a natural person.

30. "Competent court" means a court in a Contracting State that, according to the rules on the internal allocation of jurisdiction among the courts of that State, may exercise jurisdiction over the dispute.

Article 2. Interpretation of this Convention

In the interpretation of this Convention, regard is to be had to its international character and to the need to promote uniformity in its application and the observance of good faith in international trade.

* * *

Article 4. Applicability of defences and limits of liability

1. Any provision of this Convention that may provide a defence for, or limit the liability of, the carrier applies in any judicial or arbitral proceeding, whether founded in contract, in tort, or otherwise, that is instituted in respect of loss of, damage to, or delay in delivery of goods covered by a contract of carriage or for the breach of any other obligation under this Convention against:

(a) The carrier or a maritime performing party;

(b) The master, crew or any other person that performs services on board the ship; or

(c) Employees of the carrier or a maritime performing party.

2. Any provision of this Convention that may provide a defence for the shipper or the documentary shipper applies in any judicial or arbitral proceeding, whether founded in contract, in tort, or otherwise, that is instituted against the shipper, the documentary shipper, or their subcontractors, agents or employees.

CHAPTER 2. SCOPE OF APPLICATION

Article 5. General scope of application

1. Subject to article 6, this Convention applies to contracts of carriage in which the place of receipt and the place of delivery are in different States, and the port of loading of a sea carriage and the port of discharge of the same sea carriage are in different States, if, according to the contract of carriage, any one of the following places is located in a Contracting State:

(a) The place of receipt;

(b) The port of loading;

(c) The place of delivery; or

(d) The port of discharge.

2. This Convention applies without regard to the nationality of the vessel, the carrier, the performing parties, the shipper, the consignee, or any other interested parties.

Article 6. Specific exclusions

1. This Convention does not apply to the following contracts in liner transportation:

(a) Charterparties; and

(b) Other contracts for the use of a ship or of any space thereon.

2. This Convention does not apply to contracts of carriage in non-liner transportation except when:

(a) There is no charterparty or other contract between the parties for the use of a ship or of any space thereon; and

(b) A transport document or an electronic transport record is issued.

Article 7. Application to certain parties

Notwithstanding article 6, this Convention applies as between the carrier and the consignee, controlling party or holder that is not an original party to the charterparty or other contract of carriage excluded from the application of this Convention. However, this Convention does not apply as between the original parties to a contract of carriage excluded pursuant to article 6.

* * *

CHAPTER 4. OBLIGATIONS OF THE CARRIER

Article 11. Carriage and delivery of the goods

The carrier shall, subject to this Convention and in accordance with the terms of the contract of carriage, carry the goods to the place of destination and deliver them to the consignee.

Article 12. Period of responsibility of the carrier

1. The period of responsibility of the carrier for the goods under this Convention begins when the carrier or a performing party receives the goods for carriage and ends when the goods are delivered.

2. (a) If the law or regulations of the place of receipt require the goods to be handed over to an authority or other third party from which the carrier may collect them, the period of responsibility of the carrier begins when the carrier collects the goods from the authority or other third party.

(b) If the law or regulations of the place of delivery require the carrier to hand over the goods to an authority or other third party from which the consignee may collect them, the period of responsibility of the carrier ends when the carrier hands the goods over to the authority or other third party.

3. For the purpose of determining the carrier's period of responsibility, the parties may agree on the time and location of receipt and delivery of the goods, but a provision in a contract of carriage is void to the extent that it provides that:

(a) The time of receipt of the goods is subsequent to the beginning of their initial loading under the contract of carriage; or

(b) The time of delivery of the goods is prior to the completion of their final unloading under the contract of carriage.

Article 13. Specific obligations

1. The carrier shall during the period of its responsibility as defined in article 12 * * * properly and carefully receive, load, handle, stow, carry, keep, care for, unload and deliver the goods.

2. Notwithstanding paragraph 1 of this article, and without prejudice to the other provisions in chapter 4 and to chapters 5 to 7, the carrier and the shipper may agree that the loading, handling, stowing or unloading of the goods is to be performed by the shipper, the documentary shipper or the consignee. Such an agreement shall be referred to in the contract particulars.

Article 14. Specific obligations applicable to the voyage by sea

The carrier is bound before, at the beginning of, and during the voyage by sea to exercise due diligence to:

(a) Make and keep the ship seaworthy;

(b) Properly crew, equip and supply the ship and keep the ship so crewed, equipped and supplied throughout the voyage; and

(c) Make and keep the holds and all other parts of the ship in which the goods are carried, and any containers supplied by the carrier in or upon which the goods are carried, fit and safe for their reception, carriage and preservation.

* * *

CHAPTER 5. LIABILITY OF THE CARRIER FOR LOSS, DAMAGE OR DELAY

Article 17. Basis of liability

1. The carrier is liable for loss of or damage to the goods, as well as for delay in delivery, if the claimant proves that the loss, damage, or delay, or the event or circumstance that caused or contributed to it took place during the period of the carrier's responsibility as defined in chapter 4.

2. The carrier is relieved of all or part of its liability pursuant to paragraph 1 of this article if it proves that the cause or one of the causes of the loss, damage, or delay is not attributable to its fault or to the fault of any person referred to in article 18.

3. The carrier is also relieved of all or part of its liability pursuant to paragraph 1 of this article if, alternatively to proving the absence of fault as provided in paragraph 2 of this article, it proves that one or more of the following events or circumstances caused or contributed to the loss, damage, or delay:

(a) Act of God;

(b) Perils, dangers, and accidents of the sea or other navigable waters;

(c) War, hostilities, armed conflict, piracy, terrorism, riots, and civil commotions;

(d) Quarantine restrictions; interference by or impediments created by governments, public authorities, rulers, or people including detention, arrest, or seizure not attributable to the carrier or any person referred to in article 18;

(e) Strikes, lockouts, stoppages, or restraints of labour;

(f) Fire on the ship;

(g) Latent defects not discoverable by due diligence;

(h) Act or omission of the shipper, the documentary shipper, the controlling party, or any other person for whose acts the shipper or the documentary shipper is liable pursuant to article 33 or 34;

(i) Loading, handling, stowing, or unloading of the goods performed pursuant to an agreement in accordance with article 13, paragraph 2, unless the carrier or a performing party performs such activity on behalf of the shipper, the documentary shipper or the consignee;

(j) Wastage in bulk or weight or any other loss or damage arising from inherent defect, quality, or vice of the goods;

(k) Insufficiency or defective condition of packing or marking not performed by or on behalf of the carrier;

(l) Saving or attempting to save life at sea;

(m) Reasonable measures to save or attempt to save property at sea;

(n) Reasonable measures to avoid or attempt to avoid damage to the environment; or

(o) Acts of the carrier in pursuance of the powers conferred by articles 15 and 16.

4. Notwithstanding paragraph 3 of this article, the carrier is liable for all or part of the loss, damage, or delay:

(a) If the claimant proves that the fault of the carrier or of a person referred to in article 18 caused or contributed to the event or circumstance on which the carrier relies; or

(b) If the claimant proves that an event or circumstance not listed in paragraph 3 of this article contributed to the loss, damage, or delay, and the carrier cannot prove that this event or circumstance is not attributable to its fault or to the fault of any person referred to in article 18.

5. The carrier is also liable, notwithstanding paragraph 3 of this article, for all or part of the loss, damage, or delay if:

(a) The claimant proves that the loss, damage, or delay was or was probably caused by or contributed to by (i) the unseaworthiness of the ship; (ii) the improper crewing, equipping, and supplying of the ship; or (iii) the fact that the holds or other parts of the ship in which the goods are carried, or any containers supplied by the carrier in or upon which the goods are carried, were not fit and safe for reception, carriage, and preservation of the goods; and

(b) The carrier is unable to prove either that: (i) none of the events or circumstances referred to in subparagraph 5 (a) of this article caused the loss, damage, or delay; or (ii) that it complied with its obligation to exercise due diligence pursuant to article 14.

6. When the carrier is relieved of part of its liability pursuant to this article, the carrier is liable only for that part of the loss, damage or delay that is attributable to the event or circumstance for which it is liable pursuant to this article.

Article 18. Liability of the carrier for other persons

The carrier is liable for the breach of its obligations under this Convention caused by the acts or omissions of:

(a) Any performing party;

(b) The master or crew of the ship;

(c) Employees of the carrier or a performing party; or

(d) Any other person that performs or undertakes to perform any of the carrier's obligations under the contract of carriage, to the extent that the person acts, either directly or indirectly, at the carrier's request or under the carrier's supervision or control.

Article 19. Liability of maritime performing parties

1. A maritime performing party is subject to the obligations and liabilities imposed on the carrier under this Convention and is entitled to the carrier's defences and limits of liability as provided for in this Convention if:

(a) The maritime performing party received the goods for carriage in a Contracting State, or delivered them in a Contracting State, or performed its activities with respect to the goods in a port in a Contracting State; and

(b) The occurrence that caused the loss, damage or delay took place: (i) during the period between the arrival of the goods at the port of loading of the ship and their departure from the port of discharge from the ship; (ii) while the maritime performing party had custody of the goods; or (iii) at any other time to the extent that it was participating in the performance of any of the activities contemplated by the contract of carriage.

2. If the carrier agrees to assume obligations other than those imposed on the carrier under this Convention, or agrees that the limits of its liability are higher than the limits specified under this Convention, a maritime performing party is not bound by this agreement unless it expressly agrees to accept such obligations or such higher limits.

3. A maritime performing party is liable for the breach of its obligations under this Convention caused by the acts or omissions of any person to which it has entrusted the performance of any of the carrier's obligations under the contract of carriage under the conditions set out in paragraph 1 of this article.

4. Nothing in this Convention imposes liability on the master or crew of the ship or on an employee of the carrier or of a maritime performing party.

* * *

Article 23. Notice in case of loss, damage or delay

1. The carrier is presumed, in absence of proof to the contrary, to have delivered the goods according to their description in the contract particulars unless notice of loss of or damage to the goods, indicating the general nature of such loss or damage, was given to the carrier or the performing party that delivered the goods before or at the time of the delivery, or, if the loss or damage is not apparent, within seven working days at the place of delivery after the delivery of the goods.

2. Failure to provide the notice referred to in this article to the carrier or the performing party shall not affect the right to claim compensation for loss of or damage to the goods under this Convention, nor shall it affect the allocation of the burden of proof set out in article 17.

3. The notice referred to in this article is not required in respect of loss or damage that is ascertained in a joint inspection of the goods by the person to which they have been delivered and the carrier or the maritime performing party against which liability is being asserted.

4. No compensation in respect of delay is payable unless notice of loss due to delay was given to the carrier within twenty-one consecutive days of delivery of the goods.

5. When the notice referred to in this article is given to the performing party that delivered the goods, it has the same effect as if that notice was given to the carrier, and notice given to the carrier has the same effect as a notice given to a maritime performing party.

6. In the case of any actual or apprehended loss or damage, the parties to the dispute shall give all reasonable facilities to each other for inspecting and tallying the goods and shall provide access to records and documents relevant to the carriage of the goods.

CHAPTER 6. ADDITIONAL PROVISIONS RELATING TO PARTICULAR STAGES OF CARRIAGE

Article 24. Deviation

When pursuant to applicable law a deviation constitutes a breach of the carrier's obligations, such deviation of itself shall not deprive the carrier or a maritime performing party of any defence or limitation of this Convention, except to the extent provided in article 61.

* * *

CHAPTER 8. TRANSPORT DOCUMENTS AND ELECTRONIC
TRANSPORT RECORDS

Article 35. Issuance of the transport document or the electronic transport record

Unless the shipper and the carrier have agreed not to use a transport document or an electronic transport record, or it is the custom, usage or practice of the trade not to use one, upon delivery of the goods for carriage to the carrier or performing party, the shipper or, if the shipper consents, the documentary shipper, is entitled to obtain from the carrier, at the shipper's option:

(a) A non-negotiable transport document or, subject to article 8, subparagraph (a), a non-negotiable electronic transport record; or

(b) An appropriate negotiable transport document or, subject to article 8, subparagraph (a), a negotiable electronic transport record, unless the shipper and the carrier have agreed not to use a negotiable transport document or negotiable electronic transport record, or it is the custom, usage or practice of the trade not to use one.

Article 36. Contract particulars

1. The contract particulars in the transport document or electronic transport record referred to in article 35 shall include the following information, as furnished by the shipper:

(a) A description of the goods as appropriate for the transport;

(b) The leading marks necessary for identification of the goods;

(c) The number of packages or pieces, or the quantity of goods; and

(d) The weight of the goods, if furnished by the shipper.

2. The contract particulars in the transport document or electronic transport record referred to in article 35 shall also include:

(a) A statement of the apparent order and condition of the goods at the time the carrier or a performing party receives them for carriage;

(b) The name and address of the carrier;

(c) The date on which the carrier or a performing party received the goods, or on which the goods were loaded on board the ship, or on which the transport document or electronic transport record was issued; and

(d) If the transport document is negotiable, the number of originals of the negotiable transport document, when more than one original is issued.

3. The contract particulars in the transport document or electronic transport record referred to in article 35 shall further include:

(a) The name and address of the consignee, if named by the shipper;

(b) The name of a ship, if specified in the contract of carriage;

(c) The place of receipt and, if known to the carrier, the place of delivery; and

(d) The port of loading and the port of discharge, if specified in the contract of carriage.

4. For the purposes of this article, the phrase "apparent order and condition of the goods" in subparagraph 2 (a) of this article refers to the order and condition of the goods based on:

(a) A reasonable external inspection of the goods as packaged at the time the shipper delivers them to the carrier or a performing party; and

(b) Any additional inspection that the carrier or a performing party actually performs before issuing the transport document or electronic transport record.

* * *

Article 39. Deficiencies in the contract particulars

1. The absence or inaccuracy of one or more of the contract particulars referred to in article 36, paragraphs 1, 2 or 3, does not of itself affect the legal character or validity of the transport document or of the electronic transport record.

2. If the contract particulars include the date but fail to indicate its significance, the date is deemed to be:

(a) The date on which all of the goods indicated in the transport document or electronic transport record were loaded on board the ship, if the contract particulars indicate that the goods have been loaded on board a ship; or

(b) The date on which the carrier or a performing party received the goods, if the contract particulars do not indicate that the goods have been loaded on board a ship.

3. If the contract particulars fail to state the apparent order and condition of the goods at the time the carrier or a performing party receives them, the contract particulars are deemed to have stated that the goods were in apparent good order and condition at the time the carrier or a performing party received them.

Article 40. Qualifying the information relating to the goods in the contract particulars

1. The carrier shall qualify the information referred to in article 36, paragraph 1 to indicate that the carrier does not assume responsibility for the accuracy of the information furnished by the shipper if:

(a) The carrier has actual knowledge that any material statement in the transport document or electronic transport record is false or misleading; or

(b) The carrier has reasonable grounds to believe that a material statement in the transport document or electronic transport record is false or misleading.

2. Without prejudice to paragraph 1 of this article, the carrier may qualify the information referred to in article 36, paragraph 1 in the circumstances and in the manner set out in paragraphs 3 and 4 of this article to indicate that the carrier does not assume responsibility for the accuracy of the information furnished by the shipper.

3. When the goods are not delivered for carriage to the carrier or a performing party in a closed container or vehicle, or when they are delivered in a closed container or vehicle and the carrier or a performing party actually inspects them, the carrier may qualify the information referred to in article 36, paragraph 1, if:

(a) The carrier had no physically practicable or commercially reasonable means of checking the information furnished by the shipper, in which case it may indicate which information it was unable to check; or

(b) The carrier has reasonable grounds to believe the information furnished by the shipper to be inaccurate, in which case it may include a clause providing what it reasonably considers accurate information.

4. When the goods are delivered for carriage to the carrier or a performing party in a closed container or vehicle, the carrier may qualify the information referred to in:

(a) Article 36, subparagraphs 1 (a), (b), or (c), if:

(i) The goods inside the container or vehicle have not actually been inspected by the carrier or a performing party; and

(ii) Neither the carrier nor a performing party otherwise has actual knowledge of its contents before issuing the transport document or the electronic transport record; and

(b) Article 36, subparagraph 1 (d), if:

(i) Neither the carrier nor a performing party weighed the container or vehicle, and the shipper and the carrier had not agreed prior to the shipment that the container or vehicle would be weighed and the weight would be included in the contract particulars; or

(ii) There was no physically practicable or commercially reasonable means of checking the weight of the container or vehicle.

Article 41. Evidentiary effect of the contract particulars

Except to the extent that the contract particulars have been qualified in the circumstances and in the manner set out in article 40:

(a) A transport document or an electronic transport record is prima facie evidence of the carrier's receipt of the goods as stated in the contract particulars;

(b) Proof to the contrary by the carrier in respect of any contract particulars shall not be admissible, when such contract particulars are included in:

(i) A negotiable transport document or a negotiable electronic transport record that is transferred to a third party acting in good faith; or

(ii) A non-negotiable transport document that indicates that it must be surrendered in order to obtain delivery of the goods and is transferred to the consignee acting in good faith.

(c) Proof to the contrary by the carrier shall not be admissible against a consignee that in good faith has acted in reliance on any of the following contract particulars included in a non-negotiable transport document or a non-negotiable electronic transport record:

(i) The contract particulars referred to in article 36, paragraph 1, when such contract particulars are furnished by the carrier;

(ii) The number, type and identifying numbers of the containers, but not the identifying numbers of the container seals; and

(iii) The contract particulars referred to in article 36, paragraph 2.

* * *

CHAPTER 12. LIMITS OF LIABILITY

Article 59. Limits of liability

1. Subject to articles 60 and 61, paragraph 1, the carrier's liability for breaches of its obligations under this Convention is limited to 875 units of account per package or other shipping unit, or 3 units of account per kilogram of the gross weight of the goods that are the subject of the claim or dispute, whichever amount is the higher, except when the value of the goods has been declared by the shipper and included in the contract particulars, or when a higher amount than the amount of limitation of liability set out in this article has been agreed upon between the carrier and the shipper.

2. When goods are carried in or on a container, pallet or similar article of transport used to consolidate goods, or in or on a vehicle, the packages or shipping units enumerated in the contract particulars as packed in or on such article of transport or vehicle are deemed packages or shipping units. If not so enumerated, the goods in or on such article of transport or vehicle are deemed one shipping unit.

3. The unit of account referred to in this article is the Special Drawing Right as defined by the International Monetary Fund. The amounts referred to in this article are to be converted into the national currency of a State according to the value of such currency at the date of judgement or award or the date agreed upon by the parties. The value of a national currency, in terms of the Special Drawing Right, of a Contracting State that is a member of the International Monetary Fund is to be calculated in accordance with the method of valuation applied by the International Monetary Fund in effect at the date in question for its operations and transactions. The value of a national currency, in terms of the Special Drawing Right, of a Contracting State that is not a member of the International Monetary Fund is to be calculated in a manner to be determined by that State.

* * *

Article 61. Loss of the benefit of limitation of liability

1. Neither the carrier nor any of the persons referred to in article 18 is entitled to the benefit of the limitation of liability as provided in article 59, or as provided in the contract of carriage, if the claimant proves that the loss resulting from the breach of the carrier's obligation under this Convention was attributable to a personal act or omission of the person claiming a right to limit done with the intent to cause such loss or recklessly and with knowledge that such loss would probably result.

* * *

CHAPTER 13. TIME FOR SUIT

Article 62. Period of time for suit

1. No judicial or arbitral proceedings in respect of claims or disputes arising from a breach of an obligation under this Convention may be instituted after the expiration of a period of two years.

2. The period referred to in paragraph 1 of this article commences on the day on which the carrier has delivered the goods or, in cases in which no goods have been delivered or only part of the goods have been delivered, on the last day on which the goods should have been delivered. The day on which the period commences is not included in the period.

3. Notwithstanding the expiration of the period set out in paragraph 1 of this article, one party may rely on its claim as a defence or for the purpose of set-off against a claim asserted by the other party.

* * *

CHAPTER 14. JURISDICTION

Article 66. Actions against the carrier

Unless the contract of carriage contains an exclusive choice of court agreement that complies with article 67 or 72, the plaintiff has the right to institute judicial proceedings under this Convention against the carrier:

(a) In a competent court within the jurisdiction of which is situated one of the following places:

(i) The domicile of the carrier;

(ii) The place of receipt agreed in the contract of carriage;

(iii) The place of delivery agreed in the contract of carriage; or

(iv) The port where the goods are initially loaded on a ship or the port where the goods are finally discharged from a ship; or

(b) In a competent court or courts designated by an agreement between the shipper and the carrier for the purpose of deciding claims against the carrier that may arise under this Convention.

Article 67. Choice of court agreements

1. The jurisdiction of a court chosen in accordance with article 66, paragraph (b), is exclusive for disputes between the parties to the contract only if the parties so agree and the agreement conferring jurisdiction: (a) Is contained in a volume contract that clearly states the names and addresses of the parties and either (i) is individually negotiated or (ii) contains a prominent statement that there is an exclusive choice of court agreement and specifies the sections of the volume contract containing that agreement; and

(b) Clearly designates the courts of one Contracting State or one or more specific courts of one Contracting State.

2. A person that is not a party to the volume contract is bound by an exclusive choice of court agreement concluded in accordance with paragraph 1 of this article only if:

(a) The court is in one of the places designated in article 66, paragraph (a);

(b) That agreement is contained in the transport document or electronic transport record;

(c) That person is given timely and adequate notice of the court where the action shall be brought and that the jurisdiction of that court is exclusive; and

(d) The law of the court seized recognizes that that person may be bound by the exclusive choice of court agreement.

Article 68. Actions against the maritime performing party

The plaintiff has the right to institute judicial proceedings under this Convention against the maritime performing party in a competent court within the jurisdiction of which is situated one of the following places:

(a) The domicile of the maritime performing party; or

(b) The port where the goods are received by the maritime performing party, the port where the goods are delivered by the maritime performing party or the port in which the maritime performing party performs its activities with respect to the goods.

Article 69. No additional bases of jurisdiction

Subject to articles 71 and 72, no judicial proceedings under this Convention against the carrier or a maritime performing party may be instituted in a court not designated pursuant to articles 66 or 68.

Article 70. Arrest and provisional or protective measures

Nothing in this Convention affects jurisdiction with regard to provisional or protective measures, including arrest. A court in a State in which a provisional or protective measure was taken does not have jurisdiction to determine the case upon its merits unless:

(a) The requirements of this chapter are fulfilled; or

(b) An international convention that applies in that State so provides.

Article 71. Consolidation and removal of actions

1. Except when there is an exclusive choice of court agreement that is binding pursuant to articles 67 or 72, if a single action is brought against both the carrier and the maritime performing party arising out of a single occurrence, the action may be instituted only in a court designated pursuant to both article 66 and article 68. If there is no such court, such action may be instituted in a court designated pursuant to article 68, subparagraph (b), if there is such a court.

2. Except when there is an exclusive choice of court agreement that is binding pursuant to articles 67 or 72, a carrier or a maritime performing party that institutes an action seeking a declaration of non-liability or any other action that would deprive a person of its right to select the forum pursuant to article 66 or 68 shall, at the request of the defendant, withdraw that action once the defendant has chosen a court designated pursuant to article 66 or 68, whichever is applicable, where the action may be recommenced.

Article 72. Agreement after a dispute has arisen and jurisdiction when the defendant has entered an appearance

1. After a dispute has arisen, the parties to the dispute may agree to resolve it in any competent court.

2. A competent court before which a defendant appears, without contesting jurisdiction in accordance with the rules of that court, has jurisdiction.

Article 73. Recognition and enforcement

1. A decision made in one Contracting State by a court having jurisdiction under this Convention shall be recognized and enforced in another Contracting State in accordance with the law of such latter Contracting State when both States have made a declaration in accordance with article 74.

2. A court may refuse recognition and enforcement based on the grounds for the refusal of recognition and enforcement available pursuant to its law.

3. This chapter shall not affect the application of the rules of a regional economic integration organization that is a party to this Convention, as concerns the recognition or enforcement of judgements as between member States of the regional economic integration organization, whether adopted before or after this Convention.

Article 74. Application of chapter 14

The provisions of this chapter shall bind only Contracting States that declare in accordance with article 91 that they will be bound by them.

CHAPTER 15. ARBITRATION

Article 75. Arbitration agreements

1. Subject to this chapter, parties may agree that any dispute that may arise relating to the carriage of goods under this Convention shall be referred to arbitration.

2. The arbitration proceedings shall, at the option of the person asserting a claim against the carrier, take place at:

(a) Any place designated for that purpose in the arbitration agreement; or

(b) Any other place situated in a State where any of the following places is located:

(i) The domicile of the carrier;

(ii) The place of receipt agreed in the contract of carriage;

(iii) The place of delivery agreed in the contract of carriage; or

(iv) The port where the goods are initially loaded on a ship or the port where the goods are finally discharged from a ship.

3. The designation of the place of arbitration in the agreement is binding for disputes between the parties to the agreement if the agreement is contained in a volume contract that clearly states the names and addresses of the parties and either:

(a) Is individually negotiated; or

(b) Contains a prominent statement that there is an arbitration agreement and specifies the sections of the volume contract containing the arbitration agreement.

4. When an arbitration agreement has been concluded in accordance with paragraph 3 of this article, a person that is not a party to the volume contract is bound by the designation of the place of arbitration in that agreement only if:

(a) The place of arbitration designated in the agreement is situated in one of the places referred to in subparagraph 2 (b) of this article;

(b) The agreement is contained in the transport document or electronic transport record;

(c) The person to be bound is given timely and adequate notice of the place of arbitration; and

(d) Applicable law permits that person to be bound by the arbitration agreement.

5. The provisions of paragraphs 1, 2, 3 and 4 of this article are deemed to be part of every arbitration clause or agreement, and any term of such clause or agreement to the extent that it is inconsistent therewith is void.

Article 76. Arbitration agreement in non-liner transportation

1. Nothing in this Convention affects the enforceability of an arbitration agreement in a contract of carriage in non-liner transportation to which this Convention or the provisions of this Convention apply by reason of:

(a) The application of article 7; or

(b) The parties' voluntary incorporation of this Convention in a contract of carriage that would not otherwise be subject to this Convention.

2. Notwithstanding paragraph 1 of this article, an arbitration agreement in a transport document or electronic transport record to which this Convention applies by reason of

the application of article 7 is subject to this chapter unless such a transport document or electronic transport record:

(a) Identifies the parties to and the date of the charterparty or other contract excluded from the application of this Convention by reason of the application of article 6; and

(b) Incorporates by specific reference the clause in the charterparty or other contract that contains the terms of the arbitration agreement.

Article 77. Agreement to arbitrate after a dispute has arisen

Notwithstanding the provisions of this chapter and chapter 14, after a dispute has arisen the parties to the dispute may agree to resolve it by arbitration in any place.

Article 78. Application of chapter 15

The provisions of this chapter shall bind only Contracting States that declare in accordance with article 91 that they will be bound by them.

CHAPTER 16. VALIDITY OF CONTRACTUAL TERMS

Article 79. General provisions

1. Unless otherwise provided in this Convention, any term in a contract of carriage is void to the extent that it:

(a) Directly or indirectly excludes or limits the obligations of the carrier or a maritime performing party under this Convention;

(b) Directly or indirectly excludes or limits the liability of the carrier or a maritime performing party for breach of an obligation under this Convention; or

(c) Assigns a benefit of insurance of the goods in favour of the carrier or a person referred to in article 18.

2. Unless otherwise provided in this Convention, any term in a contract of carriage is void to the extent that it:

(a) Directly or indirectly excludes, limits or increases the obligations under this Convention of the shipper, consignee, controlling party, holder or documentary shipper; or

(b) Directly or indirectly excludes, limits or increases the liability of the shipper, consignee, controlling party, holder or documentary shipper for breach of any of its obligations under this Convention.

Article 80. Special rules for volume contracts

1. Notwithstanding article 79, as between the carrier and the shipper, a volume contract to which this Convention applies may provide for greater or lesser rights, obligations and liabilities than those imposed by this Convention.

2. A derogation pursuant to paragraph 1 of this article is binding only when:

(a) The volume contract contains a prominent statement that it derogates from this Convention;

(b) The volume contract is (i) individually negotiated or (ii) prominently specifies the sections of the volume contract containing the derogations;

(c) The shipper is given an opportunity and notice of the opportunity to conclude a contract of carriage on terms and conditions that comply with this Convention without any derogation under this article; and

(d) The derogation is neither (i) incorporated by reference from another document nor (ii) included in a contract of adhesion that is not subject to negotiation.

3. A carrier's public schedule of prices and services, transport document, electronic transport record or similar document is not a volume contract pursuant to paragraph 1 of this article, but a volume contract may incorporate such documents by reference as terms of the contract.

4. Paragraph 1 of this article does not apply to rights and obligations provided in articles 14, subparagraphs (a) and (b), 29 and 32 or to liability arising from the breach thereof, nor does it apply to any liability arising from an act or omission referred to in article 61.

5. The terms of the volume contract that derogate from this Convention, if the volume contract satisfies the requirements of paragraph 2 of this article, apply between the carrier and any person other than the shipper provided that:

(a) Such person received information that prominently states that the volume contract derogates from this Convention and gave its express consent to be bound by such derogations; and

(b) Such consent is not solely set forth in a carrier's public schedule of prices and services, transport document or electronic transport record.

6. The party claiming the benefit of the derogation bears the burden of proof that the conditions for derogation have been fulfilled.